ACCLAIM FOR

Doing Democracy with Cir(

"Here is the definitive guide on circles with planners in mind. Primal and potent in equal measure, the circle is the basis for all good conversation. It is well nigh indispensable today for those practicing planning as collective communicative action—whereby common, meaning-filled places get made.

"[This book] presses many of the hot buttons for planners looking to be more relevant and effective in today's world, while also stretching minds into the realm of hearts and souls. Circles may be regarded as a conduit for tapping the precious galvanizing spirit in their communities—and (if professional planners dare admit it) in themselves.

"This is a timely call for planners to consciously "circle" their praxis . . . to realize fuller, fairer processes—and to facilitate a "democratics" that can transcend mere politics and contribute to a more just society."

> — *Ian Wight, Associate Professor, City Planning,*
> *Faculty of Architecture, University of Manitoba, Winnipeg*

"Rural communities will appreciate this comprehensive review of circles and how it will assist them in planning their future. A 'must read.'"

> — *Gary Davidson, FCIP, RPP, long-time rural planner and*
> *past president of both the Canadian Institute of Planners and*
> *the Ontario Professional Planners Institute.*

"Circles are a place where democracy occasionally breaks out. Thanks to the authors and the whole gang at Living Justice Press for putting together this wonderful book! It will be a great catalyst to enlivening a conversation that is much needed in thousands of neighborhoods across this land."

> — *Howard Vogel, Professor, Hamline University School of Law*
> *and Dispute Resolution Institute, Saint Paul, Minnesota*

"The planning profession needs more creative and effective ways to engage the public in planning for their communities. *Doing Democracy with Circles* provides not just a new method but a new philosophy about creating community collaboratively. I have experimented with circles in several planning projects, including a comprehensive plan, developing revisions to a historic preservation ordinance, and resolving a controversy over a private development proposal. I used elements of circles as well as a more pure form of circle. All worked better than any other type of public process I have tried."
— *Phoebe Kilby, Vice President, Sympoetica, Woodstock, Virginia*

"Thumbs up for bringing a proven conflict resolution technique to the planning process!"
— *Beate Bowron, FCIP, RPP, negotiator/mediator and former Director of Community Planning, City of Toronto.*

"This book explains a simple approach to public engagement that allows democracy to emerge through respectful dialogue and understanding. This is democracy for the 21st century!"
— *Kathy Wian, Coordinator, Conflict Resolution Program, University of Delaware*

"A practical approach to community engagement and consensus building."
— *Scott Tousaw, Director, Huron County Planning and Development Department, Ontario*

"For me, the circle process was a very beneficial learning experience. I developed a whole new approach to my mediation skills that I have been able to use in a wide range of everyday situations.
"The circle process I was involved in related to water quality issues. Through the circle process, I gained insight into how people who hold different perspectives view issues and why they react to them as they do. I was never able to develop this understanding, despite several years of discussions, and I probably never would have without the benefit of learning and participating in the circle process."
— *John Gillespie, Community Member*

continued on page 194

Doing Democracy with Circles

Engaging Communities in Public Planning

Jennifer Ball, Wayne Caldwell, and Kay Pranis

Foreword by John Forester

Living Justice Press
ST. PAUL, MINNESOTA

Living Justice Press
St. Paul, Minnesota 55105

*For information about permission to reproduce selections from this book,
please contact:*
  Permissions, Living Justice Press, 2093 Juliet Avenue, St. Paul, MN 55105
  Tel. (651) 695-1008 or contact permissions through our
  Web site: www.livingjusticepress.org.

Library of Congress Cataloging-in-Publication Data

Ball, Jennifer, 1969–
    Doing democracy with circles : engaging communities in public planning /
Jennifer Ball, Wayne Caldwell, and Kay Pranis ; Foreword by John Forester. —
1st ed.
        p.   cm.
    Includes bibliographical references and index.
    ISBN 978-0-9721886-6-1 (alk. paper)
    1. Local government—United States—Citizen participation. 2. Commu-
nity development—United States. 3. Political planning—United States—
Citizen participation. 4. Healing circles. 5. Political participation—United
States. I. Caldwell, Wayne (Wayne Joseph), 1957– II. Pranis, Kay. III. Title.
    JS331.B275 2009
    320.6--dc22
                                                                    2009029664
ISBN-10: 0-9721886-6-5
ISBN-13: 978-0-9721886-6-1

13 12 11 10 09   5 4 3 2 1
Copyediting by Cathy Broberg
Cover design by David Spohn
Interior design by Wendy Holdman
Printed by Sheridan Books, Ann Arbor, Michigan on Nature's Book
recycled paper

Unless otherwise indicated, all photos courtesy of the authors.

I am of the opinion that my life belongs to the community, and as long as I live, it is my privilege to do for it whatever I can. I want to be thoroughly used up when I die, for the harder I work, the more I live. Life is no "brief candle" to me. It is a sort of splendid torch that I have got hold of for a moment, and I want to make it burn as brightly as possible before handing it on to future generations.

— *George Bernard Shaw, Irish author (1814–1885)*

There are many persons ready to do what is right because in their hearts they know it is right. But they hesitate, waiting for the other fellow to make the first move—and he, in turn, waits for you. The minute a person whose work means a great deal dares to take the openhearted and courageous way, many others follow.

— *Marian Anderson, African American contralto singer (1897–1993)*

Contents

Foreword

John Forester
Cornell University

Readers beware: this little book will challenge you to get more experience than you have, to appreciate "traditional" ideas in fresh and innovative ways, and to try new approaches and techniques as well. You'll find it all deceptively simple! What, after all, could be more simple than sitting in a circle and listening? What could be more profound than sitting in a circle with others who care as much as you do—about a question, an issue, a threat, or an opportunity—and then listening together as you try to explore what really matters, what really counts, what really can happen now?

This book presents no cure-all technique and no quick fixes, no magical solutions for planning problems. But it presents an approach, a social technology, a ritual process, a do-able, understandable, non-threatening way that planners can learn along with concerned community members about issues and questions that concern them. The "circle" approach provides more path than technique, more instructive and enlightening ritual than method, more a way to bridge understanding and action than a narrow problem-solving gimmick—all because circles encourage not just voice but listening, not just initial opinions but deeper insights, not just "what I want" but "what we can do together."

Planners at many scales find themselves haunted by complexity and by conflict. Too often, awkward processes of legally mandated public hearings seem to be what public participation comes to mean: concerned and distrusting stakeholders come, in a few minutes each, to say as emphatically and seriously as they can, what they want and fear, even if in such hearings they cannot find a way to respond to others and have others respond constructively to them. These overly formal and minimally interactive public hearings might be thought of, I often suggest, as reflecting "a political design from hell": participating community members leave more angry, more resentful, less trusting, and more cynical about public planning processes than when they arrived!

As someone who's written recently about mediated and facilitated alternatives to the generally dreadful, moderated public hearing approaches—I can only welcome this striking and useful little book providing thoughtful, practical alternatives to traditional processes of public participation. Where I have stressed a more directive, interventionist role for planners as mediators "in the middle" of differing and disputing stakeholders, this book shows planners how they might play equally subtle, if less directive, roles: convening and keeping (or enabling) circle discussions of passionately involved, locally informed, interconnected stakeholders willing to share voice and views, willing to listen carefully and learn, willing to change minds and change their own minds, willing to change the world together.

This book provides no recipe for change, but clues and tips and suggestions and leads that can help planners learn in new ways and act in better ways as well.

⌀

John Forester is one of the leading planning theorists today. He has served as chair of the Department of City and Regional Planning (1998–2001) and as associate dean of the College of Architecture, Art, and Planning (1997–1998) at Cornell University in Ithaca, New York.

His research into the micropolitics of the planning process, ethics, and political deliberation explores the ways planners shape participatory processes and manage public disputes in diverse settings. He served for many years as a mediator for the Community Dispute Resolution Center of Tompkins County, has consulted for the Consensus Building Institute, and has lectured in the past several years in Seattle, Chapel Hill, Sydney, Melbourne, Helsinki, Palermo, Johannesburg, Aix en Provence, Amsterdam, and Milan.

Professor Forester's writing includes Critical Theory and Public Life *(1985),* Planning in the Face of Power *(1989), and* The Deliberative Practitioner: Encouraging Participatory Planning Processes *(1999). His most recent book is entitled,* Dealing with Differences: Dramas of Mediating Public Disputes, *published in July 2009 by Oxford University Press. He spent the 2008–2009 academic year on sabbatical leave at the University of Amsterdam's Centre for Conflict Studies.*

Acknowledgments

Many teachers and mentors have left their imprint on us in ways we cannot even recognize, much less put into words. So, we are grateful for all of the teachers who helped prepare us for the project that led to this book.

A small group of residents of a rural community on the shores of Lake Huron, the Bluewater community, inspired us to explore the use of Circles in community planning. These people later became our colleagues on the learning journey. We are extremely grateful for their patience, their willingness to take risks with us, and their wisdom. We also want to thank those who have contributed to this work through their participation in the workshops and trainings that surrounded this planning project.

We appreciate the willingness of Angie Ober, Monica Walker-Bolten, Jane Miller-Ashton, Valerie Taliman, and Randy French to share their stories with us in this book. We are also grateful to the Indian Law Resource Center for permission to reprint the article, "Renewed Liquor Licenses Violate the Sanctity of Bear Butte," from their Web site, www.indianlaw.org.

We also want to express our gratitude to Tom Daniels, Kate Hall, Heidi Hoernig, Angela Nonkes, Susanna Reid, Larry Sherman, Sarah Thomson, and Laura Weir for their support and contributions at different stages of the writing and review process.

We are deeply indebted to Denise Breton of Living Justice Press for pushing us to the edges of new thinking about the possibilities of Circles in expanding our understanding of democracy. Our heartfelt thanks also go to Mary Joy Breton, Loretta Draths, and Deb Feeny for their tireless work on the multitude of tasks necessary to produce and distribute books.

Our special thanks to John Forester for his willingness to review this book and provide a foreword. John has inspired a generation of planners with his thoughtful work in the area of participatory planning. It is our hope that this book can contribute positively to the development of democratic processes that enhance planning outcomes.

And finally we say thanks to the universe for bringing the three of us together. The process of creating this book has been a work of joy.

Doing Democracy with Circles

Can We Fulfill the Promise of Democracy?

The Circle process is, among many other things, a problem-solving method. Circles build communities; they provide support; they generate mutual understanding; they strengthen relationships; and they create spaces for healing and transformation. But what drew us as planners to the process most is their power to help people solve complex, emotionally charged, and often otherwise intractable problems.

The possibilities for using Circles to address the challenges of human life are virtually unlimited. Circles are being used in schools, workplaces, communities, and families. Circles are also used extensively in the criminal justice system to create alternatives to incarceration, especially for youth, as well as to promote positive changes for people who live or work in prisons. Circles also provide support to ex-prisoners during re-entry. These are just a few of many possible applications of Circles.

In this book, we explore the potentials for using Circles to solve the multifaceted and often intensely emotional problems that public planners face on a regular basis. We have written this book specifically for the planning practitioner, the student of planning, and the community member who seeks better public decisions. Yet it is also true that much of the information that we offer about Circles and how to adapt them to problem-solving may be useful to those who want to apply Circles for other purposes as well.

We offer our enthusiasm and experiences in using Circles for public planning by

- describing the philosophy and practice of the Circle process;
- discussing the need for the process in public planning;
- relating Circles to various aspects of planning;

- explaining how to use the process in particular planning contexts;
- linking effective planning to larger community health; and
- sharing stories that breathe life into the concept.

The Larger Frame for Choosing a Decision-Making Process

Public planning occurs within the larger frame of civil society. The dominant philosophy of government affects how we collectively approach the planning process. It sets parameters and orients us when we face decisions about who participates in government processes and how their participation is received. Our philosophy of government maps out methods for making the decisions that affect us, individually and collectively.

As a function of government, public planning is fundamentally about decision-making. As such, the everyday work of public planning raises all the questions that go with decision-making processes, such as

- Whose voices should be heard? Who has a right to weigh in?
- Which factors are relevant to consider?
- Who sets the rules and parameters of the discussion?
- How do we arrive at a final decision?

These questions, in turn, hinge on the more fundamental question: Which process should we use to make the decision?

The goal is to arrive at an outcome that is sustainable, so that everyone involved can live with it. If some people or groups are left out of the decision-making process, their interests and concerns will not be taken into account as fully, and they might be motivated to see the outcome fail. Others might not take direct action against an outcome, yet they might not participate in the first place because they do not trust the process and may have long since lost hope that public processes can work in ways that are congruent with the ideals of democracy. Folks may withdraw from public processes because they know full well from experience that their voices will not be included or heard, except perhaps as a perfunctory show of "diversity" or "inclusion" that carries little weight in the actual decision-making.

On the most fundamental level, whichever process we use directly affects, if not determines, the outcome. This is a truth we know from experience.

Models of government provide the conceptual frame for choosing decision-making processes. Government is about creating and then maintaining order and harmony among diverse human beings who live in a shared environment. Unless governments maintain their authority and legitimacy through brute force, they depend on ideals to gain public support for their existence. Democracies, for example, appeal to ideals of freedom, equality, and inclusion. In an ideal democracy, all people can participate, have their voices heard, and exercise a meaningful say about their lives.

The decision-making processes that we select reflect our fundamental understanding of government and the ideals on which that understanding is based.

Democracy: The Gap between Ideals and Practices

But there is a catch. Given the complicated creatures that we are, the ideals we talk about in government and how we practice these ideals are often not fully congruent. There is a gap, and sometimes it becomes a chasm. Our strategies for putting our ideals into practice may not measure up to the ideals we espouse or aspire to. To put it another way, the ideals that provide the government's legitimacy may not line up with the experiences that many people have who live under that government.

Nowhere is this discrepancy more obvious than in our struggles to practice democracy. Precisely because we aspire to ideals of freedom and equality, the failure to "practice what we preach" becomes all the more painful for those whose freedom and equality are violated. Because of these struggles and the experiences that go with them— justice for some, injustices for others—the word "democracy" has come to mean different things to different people.

To some, the term "democracy" calls up the ideal: equality, inclusion, having every voice heard, and fairness. Democracy offers the promise that people can have some control over their lives and can participate in making the decisions that affect them. Those who view democracy this way are those who experience democracy as more or less working for them and for most of the people they know.

To others, "democracy" means just the opposite. Centuries of majority rule has systematically excluded and oppressed minorities—and the same minorities repeatedly. Over the last several centuries, millions of people on the North American continent alone, mostly people of color, have suffered horrific injustices and even death under governments that have been characterized and promoted as democratic. When people experience "democracy" as an oppressive, violent force in their lives across generations, they are not likely to view it in positive terms.

On hearing the title of this book, for example, African American Circle trainer and keeper Gwen Chandler Rhivers commented:

> Whenever I hear a white person use the word "democracy," it scares the hell out of me. Every time we talk about a democratic process, we are talking about hurt, excluding, separatism, and creating a class of victims. To me, it says nothing about being fair or treating people equally. With what I have experienced in my life, I want nothing to do with "democracy." So if we are going to use the word, we need to spell out what it means.
>
> I believe that we can practice being better human beings and that we can create spaces where we can do that, Circles being that kind of space. But for me, democracy is about boundaries, limitations, always someone who is hurt, always someone whose voice is not being heard. It is about issues of power-over, control, and hierarchy. It is about the majority costing the minority, hurting people and getting away with it.
>
> Again, from what I have experienced, democracy is where people who speak the loudest win, where people who have the most power, money, or privilege win. It is a feel-good word that doesn't actually mean what people say it means. It just creates more harm. I would guess that the way I feel about that word "democracy" might be true for many people of color. For many of us, it does not "feel good" at all.

In spite of the obvious gap between democratic ideals and the practices of slavery, genocide, discrimination, and systemic injustices, "democracy" has remained an ideal for many Euro-based peoples. It is part of the dominant narrative, which many people of color refer to as "the white myth." As Gwen articulates, democratic ideals of equality, inclusion, and fairness have not described the experiences that many people of color have had for centuries in "democratic" societies.

With the current practice of democracy, the gap between the ideal and the reality remains to be addressed. The gap challenges us to expand our understanding of what democracy can mean in practice. The first step toward closing the gap is, of course, acknowledging that the gap exists.

How Do We Put Democracy into Practice?

"Gwen is right on the money," law professor Howard Vogel of Hamline University's School of Law and Dispute Resolution Institute (Saint Paul, Minnesota) commented when he read Gwen's words. In his view, though, her critique strikes at the heart of representative democracies, not of democracy itself. In other words, the gap arises from the strategies we choose for putting democracy into practice.

In the West, the concept of democracy is usually traced to ancient Greece. "Demos" in ancient Greek referred to the common people in the Greek city-states. "Democracy" meant that the common people, not an aristocracy or a monied elite, made the laws, set the rules, and governed how these were applied. Democracy meant that regular people—ordinary citizens—were involved in making the decisions that affected their lives. This is the general concept of democracy.

But this general concept of democracy does not specify how "the people" might go about translating democratic theory into practice. Many strategies have been used over the millennia to implement democratic ideals.

Majority rule through elected representatives is one strategy for approximating the ideal of democracy. But it is an imperfect strategy. Majority rule readily devolves into tyranny when the same majority consistently oppresses and does violence to the same minorities, and the minorities have no recourse to justice. Majority rule can become tyrannous overnight. Lynching, for example, has frequently been an act of a majority. The majority is often complicit by looking the other way on the terrorizing, unjust acts of a few. Majority rule offers no innate assurance that ideals of justice, liberty, or equality will be practiced.

Nonetheless, Euro-dominant nations have adopted representative democracies based on majority rule. It seemed a better option than instituting an all-powerful king or dictator. Moreover, European thinkers have long doubted that democracy could be practiced in full measure. "Mob rule," as some political philosophers characterized citizen participation, was viewed as dangerous. European thinkers doubted that democracy could actually work because they mistrusted that "other people"—meaning by that women and anyone who was not European—could make rational decisions for society.

The Euro-based solution has been to limit who can be involved in making decisions. Historically, white men, especially white men who owned land, gave themselves the exclusive privilege of participating in government. This fear of public involvement is still evident in some planner's practices. As technocrats, some planners may feel that they have the "right" public perspective on an issue and fear that broad-based public participation may lead to a less satisfactory outcome. As a result, some planners remain reticent to let go of control and let the people influence and contribute to the decision-making process.

Few women and few of the many people in the world who are not of European descent would view this strategy as a good solution to the problem of so-called mob rule, which citizen participation is not. Mobs go to violent excesses, because mob thinking is not balanced by dissenting or divergent voices. If a mob mentality is the concern, then bringing in as many different voices as possible promises a better solution. In fact, this is what Circles intentionally do.

Full Democracy Is Doable

European scepticism about democracy's doability was challenged when Europeans came to this continent and observed the radically democratic practices of many Native Peoples and First Nations. Chief Oren Lyons is a Faithkeeper of the Turtle Clan of the Onondaga

Nation, and a Chief of the Onondaga Nation Council of Chiefs of the Six Nations of the Iroquois Confederacy, the Haudenosaunee or "People of the Long House." He is also Associate Professor at SUNY Buffalo in the Center for the Americas. In his article in *Indian Roots of American Democracy*, he writes about the founding of the Haudenosaunee Confederacy by the Peacemaker and the impact it had on the European immigrants:

> The Great Peacemaker had established a government of absolute democracy, the constitution of the great law intertwined with the spiritual law.
>
> We then became a nation of laws. The people came of their own free will to participate in the decision-making of the national council and the Grand Council. Thus, the Peacemaker instilled in the nations the inherent rights of the individual with the process to protect and exercise these rights.
>
> Sovereignty, then, began with the individual, and all people were recognized to be free, from the very youngest to the eldest. It was recognized and provided for in the Great Law of Peace that liberty and equality demanded great moral fortitude, and it was the nature of free men to defend freedom....
>
> This is what prevailed upon this great Turtle Island at the first landfall of the white man. They found here in full flower, free nations guided by democratic principles...
>
> Sovereigns and sovereignty as understood by the Europeans related to the power of kings and queens, of royalty to rule men as they saw fit, to enslave human beings and control in total the lives and property of their subjects. Strange indeed it must have been for these immigrants to find a land with ... free people and free nations. The impact has reverberated down through history to this time.[1]

Clearly, democracy is not the exclusive invention of Europeans. Howard Vogel argues that it might not be any culture's invention but "a natural response from a human impulse to be connected in a good way." The challenge is to figure out how to stay "connected in a good way" when conflict arises.

Moreover, as a set of ideals for government, democracy is not inherently oppressive or unjust either. Quite the opposite: democracy moves us toward ideals of giving voice to those who have had no voice, engaging those who have been excluded, and empowering people to participate in making the decisions that affect their lives. Liberty and equality are core values of democracy, however inadequately they have been practiced in democracy's name. The failing is not with the concept or ideals but with the strategies used to implement them—to put democracy into action "on the ground." Mindful of the dangers, both Canada and the U.S., for example, strive to protect individuals—in principle, at least—by the Canadian Charter of Rights and Freedoms and the American Constitution and Bill of Rights.

Can Circles Narrow the Gap?

Circles offer a way to more completely fulfill the promise of democracy. As a strategy for decision-making, Circles create far greater congruity between democracy as an ideal and democracy as a practice. Circles ensure that each voice will be heard and each concern taken into account. Circles involve full participation. When Circles work, it is because all the participants are involved in shaping the process and keeping it on track. The participants, not a facilitator, hold themselves and each other accountable for how the process goes. If a gap starts forming between values and behavior, principles and practice, then the responsibility lies with each participant to do something about it.

As a long-time Circle trainer and keeper, Gwen Chandler-Rhivers commented, "Inside the Circle is the only place where I feel truly equal." Circles are the quintessential expression of democracy, if they are practiced in the fullest way. Reflecting on Gwen's comments and the history of "democracy" on this continent, Howard Vogel observed, based on his three-plus decades of teaching law, "Circles are a place where democracy occasionally breaks out." In Circles, the mutual respect that democracy's ideals generate can be experienced. Keen to see Circle-democracy break out more, Gwen posed the challenge:

How can we create a world where people are heard? How can we create a society that is more equal, fair, just, compassionate, and loving? The Circle might be a model to use to get there.

These are some of the deeper issues that form the backdrop of Circles and their application to public planning in particular, since planning is, once again, a government function. In the later chapters, we return to some of the issues surrounding democracy and how Euro-based societies have handled issues related to land use. Howard Vogel summarized five centuries of conflicts on the North American continent this way: "In the beginning was the land, and the struggle has always been about land." Circles offer a way to resolve our problems—even the most difficult ones, as struggles over land have been—in ways that more closely reflect our best ideals and values.

∼

Our Use of Stories

To build understanding, Circles intentionally draw on the power of storytelling, and the book's structure reflects this priority. We intersperse our discussion of Circles and their application to planning with stories from planning experiences. Shorter stories are peppered within the chapters that explain the Circle process and its uses. Longer stories are inserted as brief chapters of their own to provide a change in the rhythm and to take time to reflect on how Circles might be used in planning contexts. Both sets of stories aim to ground the discussion in concrete experiences.

The stories raise issues and describe opportunities. Some of these opportunities were seized upon as a chance to engage a deeper dialogue, often using Circles to do it. Other stories describe opportunities that were missed—situations where Circles might have helped. Still other stories show how Circles played a role in a wider, yet unfinished process. We do not know whether communities continued using Circles to address issues that clearly remained unresolved or whether further Circle work might have improved the outcomes. Their stories continue.

We decided to include some stories about "unfinished" Circle processes so as not to create unrealistic expectations, as if one or two Circles can solve everything. In chapter 12, in fact, we caution readers not to set their expectations too high about what any given Circle can accomplish. One of the greatest gifts of Circles is their ability to create a space of openness through listening. In that spirit, our hope is that the different stories will spur readers to consider approaching problems in different ways, so that new solutions can emerge. Can an ongoing use of Circles create a space of openness where otherwise unimagined outcomes might become possible?

Without question, Circles can transform conflicts. What begins as a source of frustration, bad feelings, factions, and despair can morph into opportunities for building understanding, being creative, and forming communities. With Circles, the center of conflict can become the center for practicing democracy to a degree that few of us have experienced anywhere else before. The ultimate outcome of a process that is more congruent with our best ideals is, we hope, a better and more sustainable world.

ONE

Why Use Circles?

When a community can draw on and trust its own inner resources to discover the validity of a new paradigm, the community is liberated from bondage to old, embedded, fixated ways of being in the world. The community is then able to embrace the creativity of chaos, the possibilities of dreams. People are empowered to imagine new ways of being, to problem-solve on a deep level. In this way, a community can truly take hold of its future—and its past. Together, the gathered people can soar with their dreams, weep over their losses, and be free to gather together beyond differences of opinion.

Rhea Y. Miller
Cloudhand, Clenched Fist

Coming to the Circle Cold

The peacemaking Circle process is new for most people, so participants often arrive uncertain about what to expect. One man who showed up for a Circle that was being held for community members to talk about water quality issues described his first Circle experience this way:

Before I got to the Circle meeting, I was quite concerned, I really was. I thought it was going to be a touchy-feely thing or a role-playing type thing. I am not into that kind of stuff, so I was a little apprehensive going into it, and I was ready to bolt at any minute when we started. But I was really, really surprised and really, really pleased at how it went.

We have been involved in some fairly active community meetings—finger-pointing, yelling, screaming. That kind of stuff doesn't achieve anything. This Circle process I felt achieved something. It's a really good way of cutting down on rhetoric and allowing people to speak and to say what they think without being, you know, wrong or shut down.

My problem in a meeting is that I tend to jump right in. I don't like waiting for someone to stop. I wait for them, but then I jump right in. But sometimes it is better to sit and think about things for a while, and this process allows for that, . . . seeing that you only get one chance to say something as the talking piece goes around the Circle. So these are two good things about Circles. It gives you time to think of a decent response to a question, and it also allows you to hear other points of view without people being interrupted. Sometimes when the talking piece gets around to you, you realize that you don't have to say anything because your question has already been answered.

Circles, Communities, and Planning

The Circle process described in this book is rooted in the tradition of talking Circles that Indigenous Peoples in North America use and have used for millennia. We are deeply indebted to those who have carried these traditions into modern times. We will discuss the Indigenous origins of Circles more fully in chapter 3, but first we want to describe what using Circles can do for planning.

Circles offer a structured form of dialogue. The idea is that we can engage in difficult conversations most fruitfully when we begin by nurturing our shared values. Setting aside time up front to build relationships based on what we have in common, Circles create a safe space for participants to express different viewpoints and strong emotions as they discuss difficult issues. The process is useful for both communicating and making decisions. From a broader perspective, Circles offer a way for communities to practice democracy—full citizen participation in making the decisions that will affect their lives— to an extent that we may not otherwise have known how to do.

Clearly, the Circle process has relevance for planning practices. Planning what will happen in a community involves bringing together many different perspectives, so that planners can make informed decisions. Whether the concern is land use, the environment, or social

The Circle promotes deep listening by participants.

issues, the planning process provides a framework for discussing the complex issues involved with change. The goal is for public-sector agencies and other groups to make decisions that lead to a desirable future—one that everyone can embrace.

The success of planning depends upon the quality of these discussions. How can community input most effectively steer decision makers, so that their decisions serve a broader public interest? Planners must design public processes that lead to an informed debate and that capture divergent interests.

Circles are an effective way to do this. They structure the dialogue so that it is inclusive and respectful; they engage residents; and they build community. More than this, they can fundamentally change planning practices. Over time, Circles have the potential to shift the mind-set of both planners and communities. By offering a new vision for the public's role in planning, Circles invite a philosophical shift in how we—planners and communities—approach everyday planning issues. They give us a concrete experience of what doing democracy can look like in a field that exists, at least ideally, to serve the public good.

Randy French is a planner and facilitator with French Planning Services (www. lakeplan.com). His recent projects include preparing municipal resource information packages, lake plans, consulting with First Nations, and facilitating workshops on Natural Heritage Areas, water quality, protecting shorelines, living with lakes, and environmental action plans. He writes:

> In many ways, Circles have been implicit in my practice for many years. I see Circles in so much of what I do. When I first started using Circles as a planning consultant in 1992, I was amazed at the ability the process had to bring people together, to help them share views, and to tackle difficult issues. Since that initial use with Circles, I have found that it transcends all of my facilitation.

Values: The Link between Planning and Circles

Embedded in the philosophy of Circles is an emphasis on values. This emphasis serves both our best ideals and pragmatic goals. When people act on shared values, the results are more likely to serve the group's vision. Values can guide us in concrete ways to form better relationships and to improve our performance within those relationships. They help us be the kind of people we most want to be, as we create the kind of world we most want to live in.

Applying our values is, therefore, a time-tested way to create mutually acceptable solutions to difficult problems. The Circle's emphasis on values serves the goals of planning in many ways. For example, the Circle's value-based approach helps

- to access strengths in participants to resolve very difficult problems peaceably and to everyone's satisfaction;
- to bridge differences between cultures, ages, genders, geographies, status, etc., since the core values of the Circle are widely understood and shared across these differences;
- to engage people on spiritual or meaning levels as well as on mental, physical, and emotional levels;

- to promote creativity;
- to reinforce healthy relationships;
- to build community to prevent misunderstandings and disputes;
- to energize a commitment to the shared vision of the project;
- to provide a way to guide and assess performance without becoming prescriptive;
- to form a unifying force across disciplines and circumstances; and
- to allow local autonomy as well as individual views while holding a common vision.

～

We assume that you will bring your own knowledge and experience to bear on what we offer and that your own use of Circles will lead to results that will be much richer than we could imagine. Our own understanding continues to evolve as we approach each new Circle and grow from the experience.

We believe that these are exciting times. The public is demanding more voice in public decisions. The political discourse of Western countries advocates the democratic model around the globe. Yet in their treatment of minority and less-than-privileged peoples, Western modern states have, as Gwen Chandler-Rhivers observed, often fallen far short of their democratic ideals. Now, many people are working hard to change these patterns by vesting their energies in grassroots, community-based, decision-making processes. Circles are one such process, since this is precisely the context from which they emerged.

The reasons for using Circles combine democratic ideals with practicality. We know that decisions made closest to those most affected are likely to be good—to achieve desirable and sustainable outcomes. We also know that process shapes outcomes. A good, inclusive process is more likely to produce outcomes that are widely supported and successful. Finally, we know that within conflict and turbulence are enormous opportunities. Our greatest challenges prompt us to deepen our understanding, to be creative, and to express our best selves.

How do we use these insights in our work? How can we gather and reflect on these possibilities, so that they can flourish in our planning processes? Using Circles has given us a way to experience the reality and power of these insights. We recognize, however, that your experience may differ from ours. We invite you to take what is useful for you and to gently set aside what is not. In this spirit, we are grateful for the opportunity to share our experiences with you.

TWO

Why Engage Communities?

Don't ask, "What's the problem?" Ask, "What's the story?"
That way, you'll find out what the problem really is.

Richard Neustadt and Ernest May[1]

What's the Story?

This advice to planning and policy analysts is practical, and it points out a major flaw of *modern* community planning. To be sure, planners have to respond to pressing public issues and balance competing economic, environmental, and social concerns. That's their job. Stress and pressures from all sides goes with the territory. Yet in the rush to find solutions, planners are often tempted to plunge into policy-making before they have taken the time to understand the whole "story." It does not matter whether they are working on a local neighborhood issue, a plan that affects an entire municipality, or a compelling need at the regional or national level. The temptation remains to bypass—or at least give short shrift to—what may be the most important input to the planning process: the perspectives of citizens, individual and collective.

The 2006 World Planners Congress held in Vancouver, British Columbia, emphasized the need to be much more intentional about engaging citizens. Planners were urged to "actively promote diversity, cultural competence and inclusivity" and to "work to ensure human dignity with social equity and justice for all." Most planners agree with the standards that this challenge affirms. In practice, though, they are frequently frustrated with the results of conventional approaches to bringing in the public. Public participation often means getting caught up in heated emotions. Planning issues can be very divisive, and communications often break down completely. Engaging the public seems like asking for trouble.

Housing subdivisions involve decisions around sewer and water, roads, and park space, all of which are part of the planning work.

Using the Circle process offers an alternative strategy. Circles engage the public in a way that builds relationships, develops understanding, and diffuses power imbalances. Because they hold a space that can include widely divergent viewpoints, Circles offer a way to generate a broad base of public support for planning initiatives. They can even bring consensual decision-making within reach. For these reasons, we have come to believe that Circles can play a critically important role in the planning process.

Planning's Basic Job

What does planning involve? One textbook definition states:

> Planning is the deliberate social or organizational activity of developing an optimal strategy of future action to achieve a desired set of goals, for solving novel problems in complex contexts, [that is] attended by the power and intention to commit resources and to act as necessary to implement the chosen strategy.[2]

Textbook definitions such as this one are often challenging to understand, but the concept of planning could not be more basic to human societies. Planning is about working for the public good, especially as we do things that affect those around us. It is about managing change and influencing the decisions we make today, so that we do not regret them in the future.

Employed by the public, planners are responsible for overseeing this change process. In most cases, planning is about deciding how to use land and develop communities. To be successful, these decisions must incorporate a wide range of social, economic, and environmental perspectives. And they occur on various scales, from neighborhoods, municipalities, and regions to provinces, states, and national governments as well as on international levels. In this book, we give examples of how Circles can be used for planning primarily in neighborhoods and municipalities.

Strong Emotions Go with the Territory

Change at the community level tends to imply that some aspect of an individual's life is being affected: a new building is going up; someone's livelihood is being threatened; property owners' peace and ability to enjoy their property are being compromised; or environmental threats or dangers to personal well-being are increasing. These examples show why stress and strong emotions accompany planning issues. Planners often find themselves in the middle of intensely emotional conflicts, and it is no small challenge for them to handle the emotional responses, much less the reasons behind them.

One coping mechanism we as planners use is to try to "sanitize" the issues—to strip away the emotional component. We develop an "objective" response and detach ourselves from the emotions. We might even fall into the trap of dismissing the emotions. We might describe them as an irrational response, a knee-jerk resistance to change of any kind, or perhaps a NIMBY (Not In My Back Yard) form of parochialism.

Yet to do so is to ignore the fact that emotions often reveal core values that participants in the planning process hold. They may also point to a history—individual or collective—that has not been acknowledged but relates to what is happening. The challenge and opportunity for us as planners is to recognize, respect, and respond to these emotions. We need to listen to the messages embedded in emotions, so that the wisdom they carry—however confusingly they may do it—can potentially enhance the outcomes of our planning work.

The following story taken from our years in planning illustrates this point:

> *The issue seemed straightforward enough. The funeral home in a village of 1,200 people had burned down. The owners wanted to relocate the business in a refurbished home in a residential area that was still on the main street. Because the village was small, planners estimated that there would be no more than fifteen to twenty funerals per year. Funerals provide a service that folks tend to view as required, and this particular land use had traditionally been located in residential areas. The proposal did, however, require rezoning. The initial planning analysis looked at traffic, parking, and compatibility issues. The planner concluded that the new location would have minimal impact. At the required public meeting, however, he realized that he had completely misread the situation. A delegation of fifteen to twenty people vigorously opposed the change. They were mainly concerned about traffic, parking, and compatibility.*
>
> *Following the public meeting, the planner reported the two positions to the town council, which chose to adopt the proposed change. The neighbors subsequently appealed to a provincial tribunal that mediates planning disputes. Following a review of the planning evidence, this tribunal agreed with the town council. The citizens probably went away feeling that they had not been heard.*
>
> *What seemed like a straightforward decision became complex, expensive, and full of conflict. Why did these members of the public come to a conclusion that was the exact opposite of what the planner and the municipality had concluded? How was it that an understanding between the two parties could not be built? How could the issue have been allowed to persist with such hard feelings on both sides when an open dialogue may have resolved it at an early stage?*

Such signs convey the depth of the emotions generated around some of the issues that planners face.

Another planner shared an intense experience from early in his career as a local planner:

> I had already attended many meetings with this particular municipal council. The atmosphere was one of constant tension, because the municipality was moving—somewhat reluctantly— towards developing a new community plan. The council was reluctant to engage in the process, because they were not convinced about the merits of planning. They were going forward only because they were feeling pressure from the upper levels of government to develop an appropriate land-use policy. I felt some tension directed toward me as well, because the council perceived me as an advocate for restrictions and regulations that they would be just as happy to do without. In spite of all this, though, I felt that I had developed a positive rapport with the municipal council.
>
> We had gone through the stage of involving the public, and we were making progress, I thought, on developing a plan that the council could endorse. But then at a meeting, after an intense discussion over the land division policy, one of the elected municipal

council members suddenly got very upset and challenged me to a fight. He even invited me outside to have it out. I was flabbergasted. After I gathered my senses, I appealed as diplomatically as I could to the rest of council to help us stay focused on the issue and away from conflicts between personalities.

Sitting in my car later, I had a flood of emotions. I realized that I had never felt so personally affronted. My personal security had been threatened, and my sensibilities and belief in people had been shaken to the core. I could not understand why the councillor had had such an irrational reaction to what I was saying. I didn't understand where the challenge had come from. It did not seem logical at all to me given our previous discussions.

The next day, I discovered the reason. When I spoke to the town clerk, I learned that the councillor had just been told that his daughter had cancer.

In hindsight, I struggled with what I could have done differently. The one thing I knew for sure was how important it is to build trust and understanding and to focus on building good relationships. Figuring out how to do this is another question.

While the emotions in this case did not arise from the planning issue itself, this experience does illustrate how strong emotions can come in from any source and affect the planning work. It also underscores the need to use a process, such as Circles, that has the capacity to acknowledge emotions as they arise and to respect all the dimensions of thought, emotions, and experiences that people bring to the planning work. Whenever planners engage communities, experiences such as this are possible.

After attending public meetings and other community processes, many planners come away shaking their heads. The process simply did not work. Angry voices, accusations, meetings flying out of control, an absence of respect, all leading to a breakdown in communication: these experiences are not uncommon for many people in the planning profession. These experiences, combined with the lack of constructive methods for resolving differences, lead planners not to engage communities as readily as they otherwise might. Yet the contributions that communities could make are lost as a result. Consider another example:

These signs capture the grassroots resistance efforts, showing the need for us to find ways to be in dialogue face to face rather than just in billboards and posters.

The auditorium was filled to capacity, standing room only. Police stood at the back of the room. Eight hundred people had taken the time to come, and this was just one of several meetings that the province had organized to seek input on some proposed legislation. They were considering a new planning scheme that would affect a large area of the province. The audience consisted of farmers, developers, residents, landowners, and agency staff. Many people felt that the legislation would negatively affect the current and future use of their property. Others believed that the legislation would lead to a new policy that would benefit the public for generations to come.

Given the number of people attending, participants had to register to speak. They lined up behind a microphone in the center of the room to wait their turn. A professional facilitator chaired the meeting, and two or three key provincial staff sat at a table in the front of the room. The crowd occasionally applauded a comment that seemed to resonate. While some people were matter-of-fact about what they said, the issue was obviously quite emotional for others.

Although the provincial staff made presentations on the new legislation at the outset of the meeting, the information was clearly flowing one way—from the audience to the government's representatives. Over the course of three or four hours, thirty to

*forty speakers gave their views to the province. The meeting was
orderly and generally polite, but there was an underlying tension.
The entire spectacle was fascinating to watch, but it was not ter-
ribly effective in providing "the masses" with an opportunity to
comment or to let their thoughts be known, positively or negatively. Some attendees would obviously be angry until their graves
if the legislation went through. Conversely, a huge silent majority
left without sharing their thoughts at all.*

*Reflecting on the experience, one couldn't help wondering
if there wasn't a better way. How could planning outcomes
be strengthened by integrating the diverse insights that
communities—especially those most affected by planning
decisions—have to offer?*

For most of the attendees, this process was inadequate. It did not give
them a chance to share the strong emotional ties that they have—
and that all of us have—to land, communities, and the environment.
These emotions and the stories that go with them directly express
our values, beliefs, interests, ideals, and sense of meaning and purpose in life. When we fail to acknowledge these strong and often
diverse perspectives, we cannot integrate them into the planning
process. Yet without this input that speaks to the heart of who we
are, we diminish the potentially powerful contribution that planning
can make to society.

Planning with Democratic Values

Today, most planners recognize the need for engaging the public,
even though they know the problems associated with doing so. This
trend has been building over decades. In her 1969 seminal article "A
Ladder of Citizen Participation," Sherry Arnstein stressed the need
for more inclusive processes in public planning designed to transfer
power and share it. She writes, "it is the redistribution of power that
enables the have-not citizens, presently excluded from the political
and economic processes, to be deliberately included in the future."[3]
Since then, a number of practitioners and researchers have stressed
the need for collaborative planning. The work of Scott Campbell,

Susan Fainstein, John Forester, and Judith Innes, for example, come immediately to mind.[4] The trend toward greater participation is building because it makes sense: when making decisions that affect a large number of people across time, it's a good idea to include as many of these people as possible in the planning process. Indeed, according to one general definition, collaborative planning involves "collective decision making with the participation of all those who will be affected by the decision or their representatives."[5] Susan Fainstein explains:

[T]he planner's primary function is to listen to people's stories, and assist in forging consensus among differing viewpoints. Rather than providing technocratic leadership, the planner is an experiential learner, at most providing information to participants but primarily being sensitive to points of convergence. Leadership consists not in bringing stakeholders around to a particular planning content but in getting people to agree and in ensuring that whatever the position of participants within the social-economic hierarchy, no group's interest will dominate.[6]

In this context, the Circle process offers the planning profession a new tool for engaging communities. It is not a one-way process in either direction. Instead, Circles create equal opportunities for everyone to participate. And everyone in the Circle shares responsibility for the dialogue and for building consensus. Circles can be used either as one-time, stand-alone events or in concert with other strategies for engaging the public. Certainly, whenever there is a need to develop relationships and build understanding, a Circle is a good choice.

However, planners cannot go into a Circle with a fixed idea of what the outcome should be. This is not how Circles work. In a Circle, much—if not most—of the process is given over to the participants. Keepers (or facilitators) function as part of the group and are accountable to the group in this way. They cannot impose their own agendas. If a planner can embrace this level of openness—whether or not he or she functions as the Circle keeper—then Circles can take planning to new levels of participation.

The Planner's Role in the Larger Political Process

Planners are in a unique position to work with communities. Their role is to design and deliver strategies for the public—"we the people"—to participate in shaping our own lives and futures. In fact, professional planners across the United States and Canada are bound to codes of ethics that affirm democratic values. These codes speak to the importance of engaging the community and giving voice to those whose voices are often not heard in public decision-making.

Although planners' power in the planning process is somewhat limited by the political systems in which they work, they nonetheless play a critical role in influencing the process and the resulting policies. Planners can use their power to thoughtfully and effectively work with the community. Inviting communities into the process, for example, helps planners get to the root of planning issues. They can also build mutual understanding by talking to community members about what matters most to them: their values, life stories, histories, feelings, emotions, hopes, and dreams.

It was his first substantive experience in public participation. Fresh out of the university, he was asked to take the lead in developing a new plan for a small rural township. Prior to his employment, the planning department had held kitchen meetings throughout the township, meeting with small groups of residents around the kitchen table to discuss planning issues. As he began his employment, the process was moving into a more formal stage that involved seven major, township-wide workshops. These workshops dealt with a variety of topics, from agriculture to urban development to the environment. On average, eighty to one hundred people attended these meetings.

At each of these meetings, one particular person stood out. He was stereotypical: a big, burly farmer who liked to stand at the back of the room and ask tough questions that constantly challenged the young planner. And each meeting seemed to get more difficult. Finally, the seven workshops were completed, and the planner was on to the next stage. He began to work with the council, build on the input from the meetings, and develop the new plan. The final stage of the process involved one last public meeting

Because big development projects have an impact on the surrounding neighbor-hood, a planning process is most effective and produces the best outcomes when it includes the voices of all those who will be affected.

where the new plan would be presented and discussed. As in the past, the big, burly farmer stood at the back of the room. On be-half of the council, the young planner presented the plan and then did his best to respond to a myriad of questions. Increasingly, he realized that the "farmer at the back" wasn't saying anything; he was not even heckling. The planner couldn't help wondering what he was thinking.

Finally, towards the end of the meeting, the farmer stood up. In his commanding way, he said, "This is a good plan. You listened to what we had to say."

What Circles Bring to the Planning Process

As we show throughout this book, Circles offer an alternative way to engage the public in the planning process. Even when it may not be appropriate to do a full-fledged Circle, the Circle's underlying prin-ciples can enhance many of the approaches that planners historically use. There are, in fact, a number of reasons to use Circles:

- Circles underscore how important it is to involve the public. The Circle process stresses listening, hearing all voices, being inclusive, practicing equality, and sharing power. These are all essential components of an effective public process.
- Stories, emotions, and values are intensely connected. In Circles, people can tell their stories, share their beliefs, and express their emotions in a space where they feel heard— really, deeply heard.
- The Circle process helps to establish a "safe space" by inviting participants to talk about their values. This lays a foundation for them to agree on guidelines: how the group wants to be together as they discuss difficult issues. These two phases—talking about values and agreeing on guidelines—are designed to make the dialogue more respectful and reflective. As a result, more people feel comfortable about participating, which in turn promotes a deeper understanding of the issues involved.
- Circles bring together people who have quite different views and experiences. As a result, Circles have developed ways to build relationships across differences. A good portion of a Circle meeting is spent in a "relationship-building phase." To those accustomed to "getting down to business," this time may at first seem unproductive. However, it is essential for helping the group to understand each other and to develop empathy toward others in the group.

◟

There are all sorts of possibilities for using Circles in planning. This book focuses on how they can help planners engage the public in the planning process. However, planners can also use Circles for internal administration and staff meetings. Circles can help planners coordinate projects that involve different organizations. On a broader scale, Circles can deepen the dialogue about political concerns that set the agenda for planning.

Many planners already apply a number of the Circle's concepts in their work. They do so intuitively, unaware of the connection between Circles and their standard practices. The more they understand

Serving as keeper, Wayne Caldwell and a Circle participant conclude a round on formulating guidelines.

Circle principles, the more they can apply the concepts intentionally, and the more successful their efforts to engage the public are likely to be.

Granted, the use of Circles varies according to the issue and context. Not all situations call for a Circle. However, there is an enormous potential for infusing aspects of Circles into other public processes. The traditional public meeting, for example, could start by expressing shared values and coming to an agreement about guidelines.

Moreover, Circle principles could support a philosophical shift in planners' attitudes toward the public: What role should citizens play? How can planners seek their input? Once made, how should their input be valued?

The planning field needs more robust forms of public participation. It needs processes that engage people more authentically and that work constructively with the conflicts and emotions as they arise, which they always do. These needs—combined with the promise of what greater public involvement could do for planning—have spurred us to explore Circles in our work.

CHAPTER THREE

An Overview of Circle Processes

Ancient Roots and Modern Branches

Circles have their roots in ancient traditions. Ancient cultures used processes similar to Circles to attend to the community's work, as many Indigenous Peoples around the world continue to do today. We believe the Circle is a common form of discussing issues important to a community. Circles appear to have been used throughout the ages and around the globe. The specific form of Circles we describe in this book comes most directly from various North American First Nations and Native Peoples who continue to use Circles and who integrate the Circle's core teachings into their ways of life.

However, our descriptions and suggestions also incorporate modern understandings about how to resolve conflicts and be in a good way with each other. We live in fast-changing, multicultural societies. The Circle process we use is, therefore, informed by modern experiences as well. New insights into methods of dialogue, consensus building, cross-cultural communication, change theory, and personal transformation also contribute to how we understand Circles. The process that we present balances the ancient with the contemporary, the individual with the group, and the inner with the outer self.

The idea of using Circles in public planning emerged specifically from our experiences working in several communities in Canada and the United States. In a larger sense, though, it also evolved from the Indigenous justice and the restorative justice movements. Here again, the community-based practice has a history. Around the globe, small communities are using similar processes for similar purposes, as they have done for hundreds and thousands of years. These processes are often part of the fabric of the community; they would not even be identified as a separate philosophy or practice. In these places, Circle-like processes are the way people live in community with one another. They are simply how they work out the issues of everyday life.

As a technique, the Circle organizes group communication and makes it more effective. It builds relationships, helps us make more balanced decisions, and provides a powerful means for conflict resolution. Yet the Circle is much more than a technique. It embodies a philosophy of relatedness and interconnectedness that can guide us in all circumstances. It nurtures a way of "being in Circle" that continues outside of the Circle.

As an intentional space for peacemaking, the Circle is designed to help participants bring forward their "best selves." In other words, it helps us conduct ourselves from the values that represent who we are when we are at our best. The Circle creates a protected space in which to practice this "best self"—to act from our values precisely when it might feel most risky to do. The more we practice best-self, value-guided behavior in Circles, the more we strengthen these positive habits. It becomes easier and more natural for us to carry this behavior into other parts of our lives.

The Circle's Structural Foundations

At the foundation of the Circle's structure lie two elements. First, the Circle's core structure embodies values that nurture good relationships, such as respect, equality, and inclusiveness. Second, its structure incorporates key teachings common among Indigenous communities. For example, the most basic Indigenous concept is that we are all related. In practice, this means that we are also all related to the problems around us. Bringing everyone together to address the problem, as Circles do, only makes sense. How else could we gain a whole picture of what happened and a whole solution that works for everyone?

Together, the values and ancient teachings that make Circles what they are create a strong root system that can support great weight. To use a different image, they create a container that can hold anger, frustration, joy, pain, truth, conflict, diverse worldviews, intense feelings, silence, and paradox.

1. Based on Values. To build on the values side of the Circle's foundation, participants identify values that they feel are important. They bring these values to the Circle so that the process will be healthy and the outcome will be good for everyone. Honesty, respect, openness, caring, courage, patience, and humility: these are some of the values that people want to see expressed. The exact words vary with each group, but the values raised in Circles across a wide variety of contexts are basically the same. They describe who we want to be in our best selves.

The values that express our "best self" provide the touchstone for a Circle. When, for example, keepers consider using a particular strategy during the process, they ask themselves: Will this strategy help this group of people become more aligned with their values? The Circle assumes that everyone carries best-self values. They may lie buried beneath layers of "not-best-self" habits, but they are nonetheless there.

The Circle also assumes that, if the space is safe enough, these values are likely to emerge. The values that represent the best self (an inner focus) turn out to be the same values that nurture good relationships with others (an outer focus). In Circles, the values we share are not taken for granted; they are discussed. Nor does the facilitator impose them. Having a conversation about the values we wish to hold in the Circle's collective space forms a critical part of the Circle process.

2. Reflecting Indigenous Teachings. As we said, the Indigenous roots of the Circle process shape its foundation through key teachings. These teachings often use the image of a circle as a metaphor for how the universe operates. For many Indigenous Peoples, the circle as a symbol conveys a worldview. It is a way of understanding both how the world works and how human beings can move in a natural way with the world. The following teachings are an integral part of that worldview and, therefore, an integral part of the Circle space:

- Everything is connected: "we are all related."
- Though everything is connected, the universe also has distinct parts, and it is important for these parts to be in balance.
- Every part of the universe contributes to the whole; each part has a role, a contribution, and is equally valuable.

The concept that everything is connected has profound implications. For human relationships, it means that it is not possible to drop out, kick out, or get rid of anyone. The idea also spurs us to ask: How can we be good relatives to each other? This interconnectedness applies not just to humans but also to all aspects of creation.

Interconnectedness also means it is impossible for us to be in an objective position. We cannot remove ourselves from affecting those we deal with and what we observe. Wherever we are, we are always in a web of relationships. No matter how far back we try to step, we are still connected.

It also suggests that our fates are intertwined: what happens to one affects what happens to others. Ultimately, we cannot benefit from harming others. Our relatedness urges us to look to the well-being of everyone. To this end, Circles encourage us to act from our responsibilities to each other. A group characteristic attributed to Canada geese is that, whenever a goose is ill or has been injured, two others will stay with the hurt goose until it dies or can fly again. Circles inspire this same commitment to participants: no one can be abandoned.

The Indigenous teaching about balance applies to many aspects of the Circle. To start, it speaks to who we are and how we understand our nature. Indigenous teachings describe humans as having mental, physical, emotional, and spiritual or meaning-based aspects to who we are. This fourfold nature applies not only to individuals but also to communities. Fullness in our lives and relationships requires that all elements have their place; none can be left out or ignored. Based on this teaching, the Circle invites us to participate as whole beings. We bring our mental, physical, emotional, and spiritual/meaningful experiences into the Circle space. No matter how intense an experience may be, we can trust the Circle to hold in balance the complexities of who we are in all these dimensions. As participants, we may speak our truth in each of these areas, but we may not assume that what we express is true for anyone else.

Equality is another way that the principle of balance operates in a Circle. Whenever a person or group has more power, things are out of balance. Within the Circle, each participant has equal voice.

Circles also maintain a balance between individual and community interests. The Circle attends to the well-being of the group as a collective, but it also pays attention to the well-being of participants as individuals. The Circle helps individuals see how their behavior affects the collective. In turn, it helps the community see how its behavior affects individuals.

Circles also invite a balance between outer and inner work. They give us powerful experiences of connecting with others, yet they also give us powerful experiences of connecting with ourselves. By encouraging both an inner connection with one's self and an outer connection with others, Circles support a healthy balance in how we interact.

Another core assumption of Circles based on Indigenous teachings affirms the inherent dignity and worth of each participant. Each person is assumed to have gifts to offer to the Circle. No participant is more important than any other. Caroline Westerhoff captures this idea with two assertions: "First, we are indispensable.... Second, every other person on this globe is indispensable also." On this basis, she says, "Third, we are obliged to call forth and to encourage the differences in our companions along the way." This is precisely how the Circle holds each participant: each person is unique and indispensable.

Shared values and ancient teachings infuse every aspect of the Circle process. They shape the attitude of the keeper, and they define the space that the keeper strives to create among participants. The values and teachings provide a vision for the group of what is possible.

When participants first arrive, they are sometimes not at an inner place where they can imagine being in a good way with most anyone. Best-self values and teachings about connectedness or balance may not be foremost in their minds. The Circle's job is precisely to help them move in these directions from whatever place they were in when they entered. Each step of the Circle process works toward building the capacity of participants to act according to the values and teachings. To support this shift, the Circle process models these foundations in every way possible.

The Six Structural Elements of Circles

The space created in a Circle is built upon six structural elements. As tools, these elements create a space for honest, respectful dialogue

COLLECTIVE ACTION

Figure 3.1

Community Building

Connection

Healing

Ceremony
Talking Piece
Guidelines
Storytelling
Circle Keeping
Consensus

Shared Values

Indigenous Teachings

that honors each voice and nurtures relationships. Keepers use these six structural elements as ways to make the values and teachings more concrete and workable.

Ceremony. Circles use some form of ceremony to mark the opening and closing of the special space of the Circle. Within this space, participants are asked to be more mindful of the core values that define the best in them and to act according to these values. For most people, this requires dropping masks and protections; it feels vulnerable. Yet because everyone else in the Circle is making the same commitment, it becomes safe to do so. Since this level of safety is not present in most social spaces, it is important to clearly define when that safe space begins and when it ends.

The opening ceremony helps participants to relax, to release anxieties not related to the Circle, to focus on their inner state, to be mindful of their interconnectedness, and to open themselves to positive possibilities. Closing ceremonies honor the contributions of the group and remind participants once again of their connectedness to one another and the larger world. Opening and closing ceremonies vary considerably and are designed to fit the particular group. Some are simple, some elaborate. Thoughtful readings, deep breathing, music, body movement, contemplating images or photographs, and silence are ways that keepers often use to open or close a Circle.

Talking piece. The talking piece is an object that has meaning to the group and that is passed from person to person around the circle. Only the person holding the talking piece may speak. This person has the undivided attention of everyone else in the Circle and can speak without interruption. The use of a talking piece creates space for the full expression of emotions, deeper listening, thoughtful reflection, and an unrushed pace. While the talking piece creates space for people to talk who might otherwise be hesitant to speak in a group, it never requires the holder to speak. By promoting profound listening and respectful speaking, a talking piece creates the sense of safety that people need to express difficult truths.

Guidelines. Circles use a self-governing process. Everyone takes part in creating the behavioral expectations—the guidelines—for how the group will interact. And participants do this by consensus. Because the group agrees on which guidelines to follow, everyone shares in the responsibility for applying them. The job of protecting the quality of the collective space belongs to all the participants.

Storytelling. "Sharing stories is an essential source of the power of Circles," says Barry Stuart, a retired judge from Yukon, Canada, and a

The talking piece focuses the Circle participants' attention on the speaker.

leading proponent of the peacemaking Circle process as we describe it in this book. Circles build relationships, explore issues, and bring wisdom as the Circle members share their life experiences. Telling our stories is a powerful way to transform relationships. It allows participants to see one another in a more human way. And it often breaks down assumptions that participants might have made about each other that block good communication.

The Circle invites participants to share those parts of their personal stories that relate to the purpose of the Circle. As Longfellow wrote, "If we could read the secret history of our enemies, we should find in each life sorrow and suffering enough to disarm all hostility." Storytelling engages the heart and spirit far more than a personal profile or bare factual information could do.

Keeper/Facilitator. The role of the keeper in a Circle is distinctly different from the role of facilitators in other group processes. Perhaps the leading difference is that Circle keepers are equal participants. People often worry that the personal views of a facilitator might sway the outcome. Many models of group dialogue address this concern with the notion of neutrality. Facilitators try to keep a clinical distance from the people and issues at hand. As much as possible, they present themselves as being unbiased, detached, and objective. The Indigenous roots of Circles offer a different response to concerns about bias. They do not ask keepers to detach emotionally from the group. Instead, the Indigenous process on which our understanding of Circles is based asks keepers to care equally about everyone involved. Keepers are caring members of the community. As such, their participation is important to the process. Because the talking piece regulates who speaks next, the facilitator has less control over the process than in other practices. Also, because all the participants agree on the guidelines, the keepers are not the ones responsible for how people behave. Everyone in the Circle shares these roles and responsibilities.

The facilitator's job is to monitor the dialogue and to bring any problems about the process to the group's attention. Most of the time, such problems are self-correcting. But even when they are not, it is not the keepers' job to figure out how to solve the problem or to fix things. Everyone, including the keepers, is responsible for working things out in a good way.

Consensus Decision-Making. When decisions are made in the Circle, they are made by consensus. Here, consensus means that everyone can live with the decision and support it. The decision may not be each person's first choice, but it must be acceptable to everyone. True consensus is only reached through a process that includes a strongly shared vision, equal voice, and relationships of trust. Circles provide all three of these conditions. Circles ground participants in shared values; they give each participant an equal voice through the use of a talking piece; and they use various means to build relationships throughout the process. As a result, coming to consensus in a Circle is not as difficult as many people would imagine.

Decisions that are made by consensus have many advantages over those made by a majority vote. On a practical level, they are much easier to implement. Everyone is committed to the decision and is on board with making it work. There are no disgruntled, opposing factions wanting to undermine the implementation or hoping that it will fail. Moreover, because the process considers all perspectives and works to integrate them, decisions made by consensus tend to

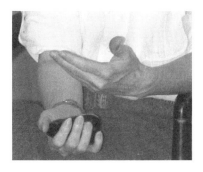

In Circles, only the person holding the talking piece speaks. The talking piece moves from person to person around the Circle. In a discussion or dialogue, the power to decide who speaks next gives the facilitator significant authority. In a Circle, this authority is in the talking piece, not in the facilitator.

be more balanced, inclusive, and fair. More of the collective wisdom goes into shaping them. As a result, they are less likely to be one-sided and more likely to be sustainable.

Other Core Characteristics of Circles

Building Relationships before Discussing Issues. Circles do not jump into talking about difficult issues. Instead, the process first gives the group time to build their relationships. In an introduction round, keepers might pose a question that invites participants to share something about themselves. The group then explores the values that each person chooses to bring to the discussion. On this basis, the group agrees on a set of guidelines that everyone accepts. After that, keepers invite a storytelling round on a topic that is loosely related to the key issue. In other words, participants spend time getting to know each other before they begin to discuss the difficult issues that have brought them together.

Sometimes building relationships can be better served if participants do not identify themselves first. It might be wiser for them to begin with exploring the values they hold in common. Imagine a judge, business executive, homeless person, ex-prisoner, young gang member, police officer, and victim of a crime all sitting in Circle. The longer they have to get to know each other as fellow human beings before they reveal their identities, the easier it may be for them to connect with each other. Stereotypes based on their experiences or on how they might be labelled would not intrude and cause them to form limiting first impressions of each other, which they then would have to overcome. Talking about values even before people introduce themselves can often be a good choice. Circles are flexible. These choices are very contextual.

The early rounds help participants connect with their common humanity. People see how their personal journeys have involved similar experiences, expectations, fears, dreams, and hopes. The opening parts of the Circle also allow participants to view each other in unexpected ways. Any assumptions they may have made about one another are gently challenged, as people listen to each other's thoughts and stories. Creating guidelines together gives the group an experience of finding common ground in spite of serious differences.

In short, Circles intentionally do *not* "get right to the issues." Circles take time for the group to create a sense of shared space and connection. This increases the level of emotional safety, which in turn allows people to go deeper into truth telling. No matter what the issue may be or how disturbing the story, the Circle grounds the dialogue in the humanity of all participants.

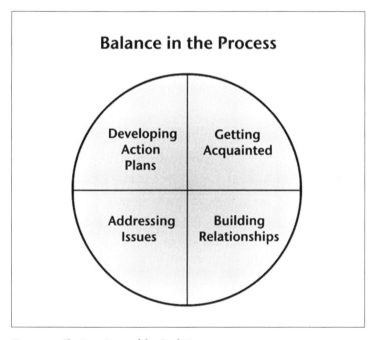

Figure 3.2: The Four Parts of the Circle Process

This diagram shows how important relationship building is to the Circle process. It is inspired by the Indigenous framework of the Medicine Wheel, which depicts a circle divided into four equal parts. Embedded in this image are many profound teachings about human beings and the universe. One of the lessons of the Medicine Wheel is that the four parts must be kept in balance.

We can use this image to describe the four parts of the Circle process. Overall, as much time should be spent on "getting acquainted" and "building relationships" as is spent on "exploring the issues" and "developing plans." Yet this balance goes against our training in Western culture. We are not accustomed to devoting time in public processes to building relationships or promoting mutual understanding. We want to be efficient and not "waste everyone's time." This explains why people new to Circles often feel enormous pressure to get to the heart of things as quickly as possible.

The Physical Format of a Circle. As the name of the process implies, the Circle's physical layout is important. Participants sit in a circle facing one another without any tables in the center. Geometry matters, and space matters. A group of people sitting in a circle without tables between them will experience a different dynamic from a group sitting in rows of chairs or even from a group sitting around a circular table.

There are many reasons for this. The geometry of a circle expresses, for example, equality. There is no head to a circle. A circle also conveys a sense of connectedness among the group. Because each participant can look directly at every other person, people have a sense of holding each other accountable as well as of being held accountable. A circle has a single focal point in the center. Putting something that relates to the issue in the center focuses the group on the purpose of the Circle and limits distractions. The lack of tables encourages people to be fully present, and it further supports an atmosphere of accountability and openness. Sitting in a circle, participants may pass the talking piece without speaking, but they cannot hide.

Shared Leadership. Circles shift responsibility for the process from the keeper to all the participants. In one way or another, each of the

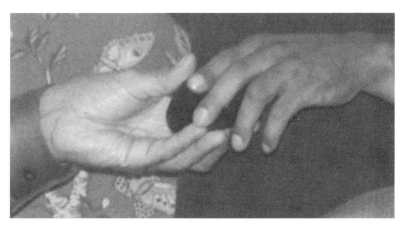

The talking piece passing from hand to hand validates the importance of every participants' voice, even if people choose to pass without speaking.

Circle's structural elements and characteristics support this shift. For example, when the group generates the values and guidelines for the Circle, the entire Circle participates in setting the expectations for behavior. As a result, participants are more likely to take responsibility for making sure that these expectations are met. They are also less likely to rely on the keepers to enforce good conduct.

So, too, when a talking piece is used, it moves around the Circle to regulate who speaks and when. This greatly reduces the role and power of the keepers. In many other group processes, the facilitator has the power to decide who has a chance to speak, and the facilitator can speak at any time. In a Circle, the keepers may speak without the talking piece, but only to address a serious challenge about the process. All the participants, not just the keepers, are responsible for the quality of the process. Because keepers sit as equals and generally speak only when the talking piece comes to them, the group is less likely to depend on them for solutions or control.

The Four Stages of the Circle Process

Using the Circle involves more than putting chairs in a circle. The Circle is a process. In fact, we capitalize the word "circle" to underscore this distinction. The complexity of the process and the importance of its stages vary enormously depending on the purpose of a Circle. While working through the stages outlined below is helpful in all types of Circles, it is most critical to pay attention to these stages in Circles that address harm or conflict or that deal with very emotional issues. The following four stages provide a useful framework for understanding the Circle process in its fullest use.

Stage 1: Determining a Circle's Suitability

Is the Circle a good choice of process for this situation? To assess the suitability of a Circle, we need to consider some questions:

- Are the key parties willing?
- Do the key parties seem motivated enough to keep going with the Circle, even if the process were to become uncomfortable or difficult?

Then there are practical issues to consider:

- Are trained keepers/facilitators available?
- Are there concerns about safety?
- Are there time constraints? Circles take time, and it is very difficult to gauge exactly how much time a Circle will require. For difficult issues, more than one Circle session may well be needed.
- If room rental and refreshments will be involved, how will these expenses be covered?

Stage 2: Preparing for the Circle

The second stage involves identifying who needs to be present, preparing the participants, researching the situation, handling the logistics, and planning for the actual Circle session. The keepers and the organizers handle these preparations together.

- To identify who needs to be there, we might ask: Who has been impacted? Who might be impacted? Who has resources, skills, or knowledge that might be needed? Who

has similar life experiences that might add insight? Who
do the key parties need for support?

- Along with inviting the key parties, we need to make sure
they are familiar with the process and that any concerns
that they may have are addressed.
- We need to gather information about the situation, so that
we understand the main issues.
- We need to choose a time and a location.
- We need to make some provisions for refreshments. In
many Indigenous cultures, sharing a potluck meal before
or after a Circle helps to build good relations.
- We need to plan the opening and closing ceremonies,
choose a talking piece, select items to put in the center as a
focal point, and draw up key questions that can be used to
initiate different rounds.
- The keepers need to take time beforehand to prepare
themselves inwardly, so that they are aligned as much as
possible with the Circle's philosophy and approach.

Stage 3: Convening All Parties in the Circle

The third stage is the Circle session itself. Keepers make sure the
room is set up, so that they are able to welcome people as they arrive. To create a warm atmosphere as well as to show concern for the
participants' physical comfort, they provide drinks and light snacks.
After the opening ceremony, the keepers initiate a number of rounds
of the talking piece. In these rounds, they invite participants to

- introduce themselves, including a brief comment about
why they came
- identify the values they want to bring to the Circle
- develop guidelines about how they want to be together and
what they can expect from each other in how they interact
- build relationships and form connections by sharing personal experiences around a theme.

After doing these basic rounds that build a sense of who the group
is and how the group wants to be together, keepers initiate further

rounds adapted to the needs of the situation. For example, they might invite participants to

- share concerns and hopes, either about life in general or about the specific situation
- express what they are feeling
- probe their views about the issue at hand and its deeper components
- generate ideas about how to address the issue
- develop points of agreement
- explore areas of consensus for specific actions
- clarify what participants have agreed to do after they leave the Circle
- reflect on what they have just experienced in the Circle and how they feel now, including whether they think another Circle would be helpful.

The keepers then close the Circle with the closing ceremony. Sometimes keepers realize that what they had planned for the closing ceremony is no longer the best choice, in which case a moment of silence or some other backup ceremony might be used instead.

Stage 4: Following Up

Circles often generate plans of action or other ideas for follow-up activities. The last stage of the Circle process involves making sure that what was agreed on in the Circle was more than just talk. The organizers and keepers must therefore

- Assess the progress that people are making on their agreements. Are all parties fulfilling their obligations? Are they honoring their commitments?
- Respond to lapses in responsibility. If participants are not following through on their agreements, why? What has changed for them? Have other problems come up?
- Adjust the agreement as needed based on new information or other developments. Do the changes warrant convening another Circle?

- Celebrate the success of whatever has been achieved, even if the situation is not yet fully resolved.

Stage 3, convening all parties, is obviously done in Circle. But Circles may also be used in other stages. For example, when key parties are polarized, the preparation stage may involve holding separate Circles with each party and their supporters (see the example in chapter 8 of the Bluewater case). The fourth stage of following up is often done in Circle as well.

Only the most complex and difficult situations will require all four stages of the Circle process as we have described them. Some uses of Circles may not need as much preparation (stage 2), or they may not need all the steps outlined for the convened Circle (stage 3). The next chapter (chapter 4) will discuss these distinctions in more detail. Chapter 6 will explore how to apply these stages to Circles that are used for public planning.

~

Circles provide a structured way to have very difficult conversations. They create an atmosphere of respect that opens participants to hearing one another in new ways. The process is flexible. Because it builds a sense of connectedness in a group, it can be used for both intervention and prevention. When Circles are used to resolve conflicts or to work through difficulties, they are very good at uncovering the underlying causes of problems and addressing them in ways that really work.

Circles are organic in their approach. They do not try to limit the discussion or isolate an event from other related experiences. The Circle dialogue is open to anything that participants feel is relevant to discuss in order to resolve conflicts, repair harm, or change conditions, so that the trouble does not arise again. The approach invites a holistic look at people and situations. It allows people to acknowledge the forces affecting their behavior that are not of their making. And it explores ways to address these larger forces, so that they and others do not have to go through similar experiences again. The very nature of Circles makes them highly effective in dealing with complex, systemic problems.

CHAPTER FOUR

"Not in My Backyard": A Transition House for Sex Offenders

BY ANGIE OBER

Angie Ober, a community member and volunteer in Oregon, tells the following story. After attending a Circle workshop, Angie decided to take a risk and use the Circle process in a situation where her community faced a difficult and emotional issue.

A friend who works at the Corrections department shared the difficulties he would soon be facing in a neighborhood where Corrections sought to establish a transition house. The home was for male sex offenders coming from prison back into the community. While local laws did not require permission from the neighborhood to set up such a house, he realized that the neighbors could make it very difficult if they opposed the house. And he expected that they would oppose it.

Having just learned about Circles, I offered to hold a Circle with the neighbors if my friend agreed to abide by the neighborhood's decision. He agreed. I went door to door in the neighborhood, introducing myself and inviting people to a meeting to discuss the transition house. Nearly everyone was eager to talk about it. Their first reaction was to be either angry or distressed at the possibility of having a house for sex offenders located in their neighborhood.

I also spent time with the offenders who would be living in the house. Individually and as a group, I walked them through the Circle process. I talked about the potential things that the neighbors could say, and then I helped them think through how they could respond respectfully. I initially talked to eight offenders. Of the eight, five agreed to participate in the Circle.

The Circle was held in the evening at the neighborhood community center to make it as easy as possible for people to attend. I greeted people as they walked in, and my anxiety began to rise as the twenty people that I had expected to show up grew to seventy. These people were ready for combat. This was the biggest Circle I had experienced, and I was alone, the sole keeper. Looking back, I think one of the most significant things that contributed to the Circle's success is that I had connected personally with almost everyone there. In spite of the strong emotions, there was already some trust.

Because so many people showed up, I arranged them so that they were sitting in a double circle. On the inside circle, I put those who would be most directly affected by the transition house: neighbors in the immediate area, probation and parole officers, the county commissioner, three of the five offenders, the offenders' support people, and the neighbors' support people. I invited everyone else to sit in the outer circle.

For the opening ceremony, I read *You Are Special*. It is a children's story about the value of people and the rewards we reap personally by building bridges and finding ways to resolve our differences. The characters in the story are "Wemmicks," carved wooden creatures who live in a village together. The Wemmicks put gray dots and yellow stars on each other. They put gray dots on a fellow Wemmick for faults and imperfections, like chipped paint or clumsiness. They get yellow stars put on them for talents or blessings, such as perfect paint or an ability to jump high. Those with gray dots sometimes found that fellow Wemmicks would put even more gray dots on them, just because they already had a few.

I presented the story as a way to help us focus on the business at hand. Reading a story gave us a chance to take a deep breath, go to a different mental world, and just relax after a long day. At the end of the story, I said, "I'm just curious. Have any of you fellow 'Wemmicks' ever felt that, for whatever reason, you were walking around with more than your fair share of gray dots? Maybe your gray dots are on display for all the world to see, or maybe you have become adept at hiding them, but you know they are there all the same." People were quiet, but I could see them thinking. I went on to share a couple of my "gray dot" experiences—things I have thought or done of which I am not proud. Then I said, "Please don't feel like you have to share, but you are in the presence of fellow 'Wemmicks,' who all have their share of gray dots."

As the talking piece moved around the circle, one woman shared that, when she was younger, the state's child protection agency removed her children from her, and she almost lost her parental rights. A man in his twenties talked about his struggle with drugs—his ongoing struggle. Another man spoke about how his drinking had cost him his family, yet the price still hadn't become high enough for him to give it up. Other people shared stories about their childhood when they felt they never measured up—they never felt smart enough, athletic enough, or just plain good enough.

After a round of sharing personal stories among those in the inner circle, I thanked everyone for coming and for being willing to grapple with this very difficult issue. I thanked them for their desire to be bridge builders and to find a way across this difficult division in the community. I said I was hopeful that, whatever the outcome, the community would benefit from coming together to share our concerns in a good way and to talk with each other with respect.

We discussed our values and agreed upon some basic guidelines for the Circle. I said up front that if at any point people were not feeling respected and safe, we would first try to resolve it by taking a break. If that did not take care of it, we would stop and reschedule the Circle for another time.

Initially people just talked about being fearful. They were concerned that if the transition house were located in their neighborhood, their property values might go down. Then one brave woman shared how she had been sexually abused as a child. Although her abuser had been a relative, thinking about this project caused her memories to resurface. What she said was very emotional, and it was probably the turning point in the Circle. Several others went on to share similar stories. Then, about two and a half hours into it, the offenders began to share their own stories of victimization from their lives. The offenders spoke not to excuse their behavior or to seek sympathy but simply to show empathy and concern for the victims in the Circle.

After a lot of deep sharing, an older man in his seventies stood up.

"I have lived here in the same house for almost fifty years," he said, "and I had no idea so many of my neighbors lived with so much pain. It seems to me we have two issues before us this evening. We need to address how we as a neighborhood can come together and get acquainted and support each other, and then we have to figure out where these young fellows are going to live. If it is in our neighborhood, what will our part be in making sure it works for everyone?"

For several minutes, it was deathly quiet. Still standing, the same elderly man said, "Well let's start here. Is there anyone in the room who thinks these young fellows don't deserve a place to live?" Everyone shook their heads no. Then he said, "It's okay even if you are the only one to say no. We need to start attending to all of us." No one spoke. Then the woman who initially shared her story of being sexually abused said, "I think we need to spend the rest of the time, if no one has any objections, finding out what the men who will live here need, what the Corrections people need, and what we need."

They decided that the home would go in. Some of the neighbors offered to help do repairs to get the home ready. Two or three of the community members who shared their stories said they were going to find a support group to begin working on their own abuse issues. One woman said, "It's about time to stop hiding and using what happened to me when I was nine years old as an excuse not to take responsibility for my life now." Then she turned to the five offenders and said, "Thank you. You have been the catalyst to get me to look at myself. I have spent months thinking I hated you and all sex offenders. In reality, I have been hating myself. Welcome to our neighborhood."

The neighbors in the Circle identified several conditions that they felt were important to their sense of safety. They requested that additional police patrols be conducted in the neighborhood. And they requested that each time a new person was going to be moved into the house that he be taken around and introduced to all the neighbors.

The transition house was there for less than three months with no problems or concerns. Then the city stepped in and announced that it had made a mistake with the zoning. The house wasn't zoned properly for this use. The neighborhood was indignant that the city was now saying that the house would have to be moved. I thought we were going to have to hold another Circle between the city and the neighborhood. If I had not witnessed it firsthand, I would never have believed that a community would fight to keep a transition house for male sex offenders in their neighborhood! The most interesting thing to me, however, is that at some point, the community stopped viewing the men as "those sex offenders." They saw them much more as fellow "Wemmicks," trying hard and having both stars and more than their fair share of gray dots.

❧

The Circle created a space where people could hear each other's concerns. By sharing their life experiences, the participants recognized a connectedness. As they moved past their fears, they were able to sort out their different needs and eventually to find ways of working together to meet them. The Circle created a sense of community that the participants had not experienced before, and it opened a space for them to talk and be together in much deeper ways. Later, they used what they had learned through the Circle to act as a community, so that the decisions of their city government were in line with what they wanted for their neighborhood.

CHAPTER FIVE

Different Types of Circles for Different Uses

Types of Circles

Because the Circle process is both flexible and powerful, non-Indigenous people are now using it for all sorts of purposes, as Indigenous Peoples have done for millennia. These purposes give rise to various types of Circles. The form of the Circle changes a bit depending on why it is being used, since not all of the elements of the Circle's structure are needed for each use.

Based on hundreds of Circle trainings, we have developed a typology of Circles. In part, listing the different types of Circles illustrates the flexibility of the process. It shows the wide range of needs and situations that Circles can address.

For those who want to organize and facilitate Circles, this typology can be helpful in another way. Different types of Circles require different levels of training—a point we will take up more fully in chapter 9. When we consider using a Circle, it helps to be clear about the Circle's purpose: What is our focus here? What is the nature of the issue that we want the Circle to address? As we move forward in organizing Circles, we have found that identifying the type of Circle that people want to use helps them sort out which elements are needed and the level of training that would be most helpful for the keepers to have.

Some of the reasons for holding a Circle include

- dialogue
- learning
- understanding
- support
- healing

- celebration and honoring
- group decision-making
- conflict-resolution
- youth development
- sentencing
- reintegration
- community-building

Each of these wide-ranging applications of Circles can be useful to planners. Here, we will give a brief description of each application, and then in chapter 9, we will expand on how these uses of Circles can serve the planning process in more specific ways.

Dialogue Circles. Dialogue Circles bring people together to explore a specific issue or topic from many perspectives. Dialogue Circles are not about reaching a consensus on a topic. Neither do they focus on the needs or issues of specific participants. They simply create a space where all voices can be heard in a respectful way, and they expose participants to a diversity of perspectives to stimulate their thoughts and reflection. Preparation is minimal. Participants usually do not need to be prepared for the Circle experience ahead of time, neither do the keepers need to do extensive background work on the issue.

Learning Circles. A learning Circle uses the Circle process for teaching or sharing information. Consensus is not a concern in this use either. Neither does a learning Circle require that individuals prepare for the Circle. And these Circles may or may not involve follow-up.

Learning Circles can play a significant role in public discourse. So many of the issues we face collectively involve complex technical, scientific, or specialized knowledge—knowledge that most of us may not have. Without this knowledge, our participation in public dialogue is limited. Learning Circles address this need. Experts in an area can be invited to a Circle to present background information on the subject at hand. If they want to participate in the Circle, then they need to be briefed about how Circles work. This briefing of the visiting experts about Circles may also serve as an opportunity for the group to go over the values and guidelines. However, speakers can also come in as guests to make an initial presentation, answer questions, and then depart, leaving it to the Circle participants to decide how best to apply the new perspectives. After such a presentation, participants would probably appreciate a break anyway, so the speaker's departure would feel natural at that time.

The Circle process can then help participants digest the information together and relate it to the issues at hand. Learning Circles empower people to work from a shared base of knowledge. Just as experts have a store of knowledge that the average citizen may not, so, too, each of us has unique experiences that bring insight and creativity to issues. Sharing knowledge engages the full potential of what everyone brings to an issue.

Another obvious use of learning Circles is in the classroom. Many teachers and professors now regularly hold their classes in a Circle format. Circles create a space for cooperative learning. They also make it possible for those who are sharing information to find out how their listeners are receiving the material. Beyond improving the flow of communication, though, learning Circles shift the entire model of learning. Instead of treating students as "blank slates" on which to download data, Circles create an organic, dialogue-based experience that honors what everyone brings to the learning process.

Circles of Understanding. Circles of understanding are dialogue Circles focused on clarifying a specific issue: Can we gain a better understanding of this difficult situation? Circles of understanding do not involve decision-making, so they are not concerned with trying to reach a consensus. Their purpose is to develop a clearer picture of the context for some behavior or the reasons behind a conflict or an event. If a Circle of understanding is gathered to bring clarity to one or more individuals about a current situation, then these individuals should be prepared for the Circle beforehand, and the keepers must make sure that they have adequate support people in attendance.

The keepers of these types of Circles need to prepare in another way as well. It is their job to see that all the perspectives necessary for a fuller understanding of the situation are represented. A Circle of understanding is not going to generate much insight if all the participants see things the same way or if some perspective, however contentious, is not adequately expressed.

Circles provide a space for participants to share what is important to them, which builds relationships as well as mutual understanding.

Support Circles. A support Circle brings key people together to support a person through a rough period or a major change in life. Support Circles often meet regularly during a given time frame. Working by consensus, support Circles may develop agreements or plans of how best to support a person, but the Circles are not necessarily involved with decision-making. Naturally, the person being supported is the one who says what feels supportive and what does not. While support Circles require a lot of organization and preparation up front, the amount of preparation for each Circle lessens as the process continues.

Healing Circles. The purpose of a healing Circle is to share the pain of a person, family, or group who has experienced trauma or loss. The aim is not to "fix" people but simply to be present with them and what they have experienced. Accordingly, although a plan may emerge for how to support those in pain after the Circle is over, it is by no means necessary. Above all, keepers and organizers need to prepare for healing Circles carefully by finding out from those who are struggling what they want and need. Otherwise, in spite of good intentions, the process could inadvertently cause more distress.

Celebration or Honoring Circles. Celebration Circles bring people together to recognize a person, group, or event. They are about sharing joy and a sense of accomplishment. Beyond making sure that participants agree to respect the talking piece, keepers of celebration Circles generally do not do rounds for generating guidelines. Arriving at a consensus is not an issue either. However, keepers may view celebrations as a chance for groups to reinforce their values. For example, they might initiate a round by asking, "What values made this achievement possible?" or "Which value best describes your feelings right now?'

Preparing for celebration Circles mostly involves logistics and invitations. People use them for birthdays, graduations, anniversaries, awards, retirements, and many other milestone events. Using Circles at these occasions deepens the experience. People come away with a sense of shared meaning and of feeling connected with everyone present that is often missing from social events.

Group Decision-Making Circles. Decision-making Circles focus on helping people reach a decision by consensus. Most likely, the participants come with very different views about what is important and what should be done. The Circle process is designed to generate a decision that incorporates everyone's concerns. For the process to be most effective, organizers put special efforts into the preparation stage. Separate Circles of understanding or community building may need to be held before everyone comes together in a Circle to make the decision. Work groups, governing boards, advisory councils, governments, schools, businesses, and families use these Circles to arrive at decisions that affect their communities.

Conflict-Resolution Circles. Conflict-resolution Circles bring disputing parties together to resolve their differences. The resolution is usually expressed in a consensus agreement. This type of Circle often requires that those who are in conflict be extensively prepared beforehand. For example, other types of Circles can be extremely helpful in preparing the parties for a conflict Circle. People may need support or healing Circles. They may need Circles of understanding to get a better picture of what is going on. Or they may simply need dialogue Circles to explore their own thoughts and feelings as well as to see what different people are thinking about the conflict.

When the parties in conflict finally come together in a Circle to try to resolve the conflict, a considerable amount of time is spent building relationships before participants begin to discuss the core issues. Conflict Circles are being used to deal with conflicts, for example, in neighborhoods, workplaces, schools, churches, prisons, and families.

Youth Development Circles. The Circle process is the same no matter who the participants are, young or old. However, it bears mentioning that one of the fastest growing areas of Circle use is with and among young people. Young people usually respond immediately to the egalitarian, respectful ways of the Circle. And young people of all economic, social, ethnic, and national backgrounds need the quality of support from both adults and peers that Circles uniquely give.

Criminologist John Braithwaite suggests that families, schools, and communities use Circles not only when problems arise but regularly to give youth ongoing support. Indeed, "youth development Circle" is his term. Circles offer youth places where they can be heard and supported in positive ways. Circles support young people as they form their personalities, develop their social skills, respond to crises, and manage their work at school.[1] Braithwaite proposes that we make Circles a permanent feature of young people's lives.

Sentencing Circles. A sentencing Circle is a community-directed process. It works in partnership with the criminal justice system to bring together all those affected by an offense. Using the Circle process, participants develop a sentencing plan that addresses the various concerns about a case. These Circles include the person who was harmed, the person who caused the harm, the family and friends of each, as well as other community members. They also include representatives from the justice system: judges, prosecutors, defense counsels, police, probation officers, and other resource professionals.

In line with the philosophy and approach of restorative justice, participants discuss the following:

1. What happened?
2. Why did it happen?
3. What has the impact been?
4. What is needed to repair the harm?
5. What must be done to prevent this from happening again?

By consensus, the Circle develops a sentence for the person who committed the crime. It may also stipulate the responsibilities of community members and justice officials as part of the agreement.

Preparing for a sentencing Circle may well involve separate Circles for those on both sides of harm before bringing everyone together. The person who suffered the harm may need healing or support Circles. The person who committed the crime may need Circles of understanding, support, and healing as well. The goal is to respond to harms in ways that address the root of the problem and that invite transformation on all sides. In a larger sense, the goal is to use such events as opportunities to build good relations, so that individuals and communities are stronger—not weaker—as a result.

Reintegration Circles. Reintegration Circles bring a person together with the community from whom he or she has been separated. Prison reentry programs use these types of Circles, but they are valuable whenever someone has been away from a group for a long time. A woman returns to her job after maternity leave; a young person comes home after college; or a soldier returns from military service: reintegration Circles offer a space for these people and their communities to reconnect. Circles address the needs and concerns that arise for people in such situations. When reintegration Circles are used to support people through major life changes, they are generally more than onetime events.

Community-Building Circles. Community-building Circles create bonds and build relationships among a group of people who have a shared interest. They are useful for people who live, work, or otherwise spend time together to check in with each other. Whether in staff meetings, classes, or families, regular talking Circles invite people to speak from a deeper place. Participants step back and reflect on things in ways they would not otherwise do. Often, critical issues emerge that no one had been thinking about. For the ongoing health of a family, organization, school, or community, community-building Circles are a potent support. They can detect sources of trouble early on and can respond preventively.

When problems do arise, a strong Circle community is already in place to deal with them. Community-building Circles rally the energies for collective action, and they inspire a sense of mutual responsibility. They do not try to reach consensus, but they may be used to prepare people for that process. Because community-building Circles do not focus on particular participants, they do not require extensive preparation.

～

These different purposes for using Circles often overlap. Most Circles have the effect of building communities, for example, and most Circles result in healing for some of those present. Distinguishing a Circle as this or that type simply refers to the primary purpose for using it. Again, a Circle process might use several types of Circles as it moves through the various stages, from deciding on a Circle's suitability to follow-up.

Different types of Circles do, however, require different degrees of training for the keepers or those who facilitate the process. If the purpose of a Circle is to bring a group to consensus on a complex issue or to work through difficult emotions, we recommend several days of Circle training. (We have provided training information in appendix 2.) However, facilitating Circles to celebrate, talk, understand an issue, or build community can be done without formal training.

For anyone keeping a Circle, it is good to remember, once again, that there is more to Circles than sitting in a circle and passing a talking piece. Circles embody a philosophy. The more both the keepers and the participants are imbued with the Circle's philosophy, the more transformative a Circle experience is likely to be. (We have provided a list of books that discuss the Circle process in appendix 3.)

Types of Circles Useful in Planning

Many of these types of Circles can be useful in planning. For example, at the beginning of the planning process, dialogue Circles can help everyone involved with a project learn about each other: who they are, what their experiences have been, and the skills they bring to the project. Learning Circles might also be important to provide the group with critical information. Early in the process, organizers can use a combination of dialogue Circles and decision-making Circles to solicit input from all interested parties and to develop a clear shared vision for the project.

Decision-making Circles can also help those who are working on the project to develop values and guidelines for how they want to work together. As the planning progresses, check-in Circles—a form of a community-building Circle—can strengthen the working relationships. They can be used for sharing information and for keeping everyone up to date on what is going on. When major planning decisions must be made, decision-making Circles make sure that everyone takes part in the process. When misunderstandings, disputes, or other difficulties arise, conflict Circles help participants resolve their differences. More than that, conflict Circles can re-energize people by renewing their sense of working toward a shared vision. Finally, when the plan or stages of it have been completed, a celebration Circle gives the group a chance to honor what they have accomplished.

Practical Uses of Circles across Society

The longer we work with Circles, the more stories people share with us about how they are using Circles in their work, families, schools, and communities. The following are just a sampling of what people are doing with Circles.

- In a transitional housing program for homeless women and children, the director used the Circle process over a period of months to involve her entire staff in designing a new program.
- The Science Museum of Minnesota used Circles as a dialogue process for groups of people who came to view an exhibit called "RACE."
- A special high school for students who are recovering from chemical dependency convenes a Circle of the

entire school whenever a student relapses. Accountability, support, and defusing anxieties that occur in a recovery community whenever one of their members relapses: the Circle addresses all of these concerns.

- An Indigenous community in Costa Rica used the Circle process to resolve a twelve-year land dispute.
- A planner used a Circle in a small "dying" village to help the community create a vision for a positive future.
- The Minnesota Department of Corrections offers the Circle process as one of the options that staff can use to resolve staff disputes and to address workplace dysfunction.
- A Milwaukee neighborhood held Circles with youth and senior citizens to reduce the fears that senior citizens had around young people.
- In a large urban area, a youth development organization uses Circles to help youth get out of gangs as well as to create dialogue among rival gang members.
- An elementary school uses Circles to resolve disputes on the playground.
- A group of family and friends used a Circle to say good-bye to a loved one who was dying.
- A church board sat in Circle with church members who were upset about a decision that the board had made.
- A suburban community uses Circles to decide on a sentence for certain types of offenders.
- The director of a community corrections department held a Circle with his entire staff to decide how to cut the budget.
- A wilderness juvenile corrections facility used Circles with staff to heal the wounds of a bitter strike of state workers.
- A small nonprofit used a Circle to develop a vision and a mission for the organization.
- The legal department of Chicago Public Schools and a coalition of community activists who wanted to reform the discipline procedures used a Circle to find common ground. Then they continued to use Circles to collaborate on changing the "Uniform Code of Discipline."
- Staff in a planning office periodically use Circles at staff

meetings to facilitate staff involvement and more equal participation.

- At St. Joseph's University in Philadelphia, one of the professors who teaches both in the law school and in the criminal justice graduate program uses the Circle process to teach all of his classes.
- A neighborhood group held a healing Circle to support the mother and siblings of a sixteen-year-old boy who was shot and killed.
- The staff of a detention facility unit conducts weekly check-in Circles to strengthen their relationships and to improve the flow of their communications.
- A few professors and some citizens who met at a law school used the Circle process to talk about starting a truth-telling process to address the state's history of genocide and forced colonization of the land's Indigenous Peoples.

∼

Like strawberry runners in a garden, Circles have spread organically to wherever humans need a better way to be in dialogue. Circles create spaces for us to express our feelings, so that we can be in healthier relationships with one another and can work through the hurts that inevitably arise. As more people learn about the Circle process and what it can do, more innovative applications of Circles will surely emerge.

 CHAPTER SIX

One Planner's First Circle—
Community Youth Development

BY MONICA WALKER-BOLTON

Monica Walker-Bolton, a practicing land-use planner who is also engaged in community development, was inspired to use a Circle in a context that was outside of her formal responsibilities. It was, though, deeply connected to her community work. This is her story.

I work in a rural area on land-use planning as well as community and economic development. One of my responsibilities is to provide support for the local manufacturing association.

We also have an organization in town that works with youth who face barriers to employment. Through the program, participants receive a weekly paycheck, and they learn skills that better prepare them for the workforce. Participants work with the program leaders to develop a personal plan for what they want to do and how they plan to get the preparation they need. While they are in the program, they work to complete the goals they have set for themselves.

Every Friday, the program invites a guest speaker to teach the youth about life skills, such as job searching. I have been a regular guest speaker for the group on this topic, telling them about the jobs that are available in the manufacturing sector and giving them tips on how to do their job search.

When I met with the youth and spoke to the program leaders, I soon realized that many of the young people in the program were facing some very difficult situations. It can be challenging for any young person to find work in a rural community. Good jobs can be few and far between. But many of the youth in this program were facing additional challenges. Drug addiction, bullying, discrimination, low access to educational opportunities, and conflicts with the law: these were some of the added hurdles that the young people faced.

Before I began using the Circle process with the youth, I found it difficult to get my message across when I would go to speak to them. The young people seemed to respond to me personally, and they said they liked the fact that I was young too, but I got the sense that they really didn't buy my message. They were not convinced that what I was saying would apply to them. I claimed that there were lots of jobs available in the manufacturing sector and that employers were finding it difficult to attract employees. Yet this had not been their experience. Too often, employers had closed the doors to them. I needed a way to be with the youth that got to the deeper issues.

Leading My First Circle

After my Circle training, I realized I had found a process that could work for these young people. Before my next invitation as a guest speaker, I told the program leaders about the Circle process. I expressed my desire to use a Circle for my next presentation, and they agreed to let me do it.

When I arrived, I used notes on a flip chart to outline some of the basic concepts about Circles to the young people. I explained that the Circle process involves coming together in a circle and using a talking piece. I described how the talking piece works: that the person holding it can speak as much or as little as he or she wants, and that no one is allowed to interrupt. And I talked about some of the pros and cons of the Circle process. For example, a positive thing about Circles is that everyone gets a chance to speak if they want to. A negative thing is that it is sometimes hard to manage time in a Circle.

I was very excited about introducing these young people to the dynamics of equality and shared leadership that the Circle embodies. I cited these as positive things as well. I explained that the shared leadership of a Circle means that all the members of the Circle are responsible for maintaining a respectful atmosphere. And all the participants help to manage the time that the Circle process takes.

In my Circle training, we learned how to establish shared guidelines for the group. The exercise we used was for people to write down on a paper plate a value that expressed how they wanted the other group members to treat them. Since I did not have much time with the youth, I decided not to go through the process of establishing shared guidelines. Instead, we all agreed to follow the basic ground rules I had written on the flip chart as our guidelines. Still, I explained how important it is that everyone feels comfortable with the guidelines and that if we had more time, we would have developed our own set for the group.

As an opening ceremony for the Circle, I adapted something that we did in our Circle training. In the training, each of us took a piece of colored yarn. As we went around the Circle, one by one we tied our individual piece of yarn to the yarn held by the person next to us, until all the yarn was joined in a circle. For the youth, I brought cool-looking ribbons and did this exercise with them. Some of them laughed nervously, while others made questioning jokes about why I was asking them to do this. But by the time we had made it around the Circle with everyone repeating this simple act, the energy in the room had changed. The participants were more focused on what we were doing as a group, and the atmosphere in the room was already more peaceful. Together, we gently laid the circle of ribbon on the coffee table in the center, and I moved on to the next part of our opening.

In preparation, I had brought a pretty red plate from home and filled it with various plastic and felt objects that I had picked up at the dollar store. For the next part of our opening, I passed the plate of objects around and invited participants to select one that they liked. I explained that this object would represent them in the center of the circle. Next, holding the talking piece, I once again described how the talking piece regulates the dialogue. When each person received the talking piece, I suggested that they say their name and then place their object on the plate in the center of our circle. Everyone did this. When the talking piece came back to me, I was pleased that we had just completed our first round of the Circle.

From my Circle training, I knew it was important for the group to have a chance to establish some shared values. For the next round, I suggested that each participant say one positive word and one negative word about the community. I reminded them that, according to the guidelines of the Circle, they could say as much or as little as they wanted when they had the talking piece, and that passing it without saying anything was okay too. Hearing each person's words gave me a lot of insight into the young people and how they saw themselves in the community. Some just said their words, while others explained why they chose the words they did. "Family," "a safe, small-town atmosphere," and "community support," for example, were cited as positive things. "Bullying," "gossip," "drugs," and "nothing to do" were cited as negative things.

I chose to do this exercise as a simple way to get the group involved in thinking about their values. I could have asked a question like "How should we treat each other in the Circle?" In this case, though, because of the time constraints, I chose to use the discussion of values as a way to move the conversation toward our subject. It was a chance for the young people to talk about how they saw themselves in relation to the community.

For the heart of our conversation, we did several rounds on the questions: "What barriers to employment do you face?" and "How are you working to overcome them?" Since this program exists to help young people deal with challenges to employment, I thought these questions would be relevant for them. So I posed the questions and passed the talking piece.

I was surprised by how quickly the young people started sharing their personal stories and challenges. In my experience with the Circle process, both in my Circle training and with this particular group, I have found that there is something about the process that draws people out. Participants start telling personal stories and expressing emotions that just don't seem to come out in other situations. One young man, for example, talked about his experience of trying to fit into the community and find work after having been in jail. I could tell that this was a very emotional topic for him, even though his voice stayed even in tone, and he was not tearful, loud, or angry.

Several participants shared emotional stories as well. Others took their time with the talking piece to give words of encouragement to their fellow group members. I later talked with one of the program leaders about this experience and how the group came together to support each other. She observed,

> The Circle isn't about debate. Instead, there is something inherent in this process with the opening, the closing, and the talking piece that brings honesty out of people. Every time

we've used this process, people have made some deep admissions. As a result, people become very supportive of each other in their responses, and it brings us together as a group. It brings out the respect we have for each other.

The Circle process has now become a great tool for me, and I use the process whenever I can. It took me out of the position of being an authority figure, which I felt uncomfortable with anyway. Instead of coming to others with "all the answers," I am able to share with them a tool that will help them discover their own questions and find their own answers. It is an amazing process, and I think participants are often surprised as well by the quality of thought and sharing that folks are able to do in Circles.

⌁

This planner continued to hold periodic dialogue Circles with the youth and so passed on the process as a tool for these young people to use in their own lives. The Circles created a space in which socially challenged, marginalized youth could experience being treated as equals and having their voices be heard and acknowledged. They could also practice what it means to share leadership and to come together in a good way to address the difficult problems they faced.

CHAPTER SEVEN

Getting Started: How to Use a Talking Circle in a Planning Process[1]

Sitting in a Circle is by far the best way to learn about the process. If you can't find a Circle near you, organizing a dialogue Circle is a great way to start. Again, Circle training is essential before trying to facilitate a Circle for a conflict, a tough group decision, or an intensely emotional situation. But facilitating a dialogue Circle is something that anyone can do with just basic knowledge of how the process works. As we said, the same is true of celebration Circles, learning Circles, Circles of understanding, and community-building Circles. Formal Circle training is recommended only for the more complex, painful, or polarized situations.

We would also like to make a note about terminology. A number of North American Indigenous Peoples refer to Circles simply as "talking Circles." We would like to follow this usage as a general descriptive term, especially for Circles that do not have to address severe conflicts or intense emotions.

In this chapter, we outline how talking Circles could be used in a typical planning context. The overall purpose of these Circles is to allow everyone to speak about a topic from his or her own experiences. Sharing perspectives increases everyone's understanding of the issue. It also allows decision makers to consider the needs and interests of people who hold differing points of view. Within a planning context, talking Circles can be used to

- check in with one another in an ongoing group, such as a group of colleagues, staff, a civic organization, a committee, an advisory board, or a project group
- reflect on a group experience, such as having attended a conference, a public meeting, or a professional development activity

- give feedback to senior planning staff or to a leader or facilitator of a group process
- provide input to decision makers
- dialogue about community or social concerns, such as the environment or low-income housing
- explore a community's response to a specific planning proposal
- exchange divergent points of view on an emotional topic, such as selecting a site for a new landfill or a group home
- seek or give community input at the various stages of developing a new policy or plan.

The rest of this chapter describes how you can organize a talking Circle around a planning issue in a community or neighborhood. The process begins, of course, with clarifying the issue that needs to be discussed: Why do you want to hold a Circle? It is useful to frame a statement of intent for the talking Circle: What is the purpose of bringing people together in a talking Circle? Then work through the following four stages of the Circle process.

Stage 1: Deciding on the Suitability of a Talking Circle

To decide whether a talking Circle is the right process for the purpose you have in mind, we suggest that you consider the following questions:

- Will the input of others be meaningful in the planning process? Will it have some role in the decision-making? If not, then a Circle is not appropriate.
- Are there people who are willing to participate? Does the topic matter to anyone? If not, then a Circle is not appropriate.
- Am I (the organizer) hoping to convince others of a particular point of view? Am I hoping to change others? Do I have an agenda for the situation that I want the Circle to promote? If so, then a Circle is not the appropriate forum.
- Am I open to hearing and respecting perspectives very different from my own? If not, then a Circle is not appropriate.

- Is the intent to be respectful of all possible participants? If not, then a Circle is not appropriate.
- Am I considering using a Circle only as a public relations strategy? If so, then a Circle is not appropriate.

By their nature, Circles are about integrity. They set high standards of respect, honesty, and transparency. They are also about inclusion and empowerment. These values are embedded in Circle philosophy as well as in every aspect of the Circle process. Those who are thinking about arranging a talking Circle need to have their motives aligned with these values. Otherwise, their intentions and the process will be in conflict.

For example, talking Circles will not ultimately be successful in a community if planners try to use them to create merely a public image of engaging the community. Those who are making the decisions must be prepared to incorporate the community's perspectives into what they decide. Neither should talking Circles be used to try to persuade a community to accept a decision that has already been made.

Naturally, Circles are equally suitable when conflicts arise. If a plan has been made and the community opposes it, a Circle is entirely appropriate.

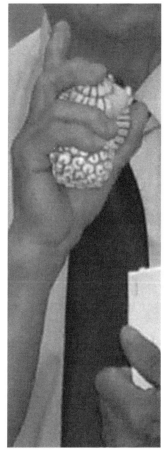

Because the talking piece regulates the flow of conversation in a Circle, the facilitator exercises less power and is more an equal member and participant in the Circle.

But in these situations, the organizers need to be transparent about the purpose of the Circle and the current situation. The presence of a conflict affects the Circle's purpose. It changes how the process is set up, and it affects everyone's expectations going into it.

As for the notion of using Circles to promote one view over others, this simply does not work. Once the talking piece starts moving around the circle, no one controls the dialogue. Any attempt to impose control will most likely be called out by one of the participants and will become a talking point in itself. When it comes to Circles, transparency and integrity about one's intentions and the reasons for holding a Circle are essential.

Considering these questions about suitability, therefore, helps those of us who organize talking Circles make sure that we are coming from an authentic place—one that is consistent with the whole idea of Circles. This is why stage 1 is so important. It involves much more than weighing logistics, data, or strategies. Deciding on suitability is also about values. The questions we posed to help organizers think about a Circle's suitability provide a check-in: Are we bringing a Circle together from a genuine, open, and honest intention? Is our goal to engage a diversity of people in exploring an issue that affects everyone in an authentic way?

Stage 2: Preparation

If you decide that a talking Circle is a suitable format for your planning process, then you can begin the preparations. And talking Circles require preparation.

- Identify potential participants. Naturally, the participants may be an existing group of people.
- Make sure to include all the interests relevant to the issue or to your purpose. The potential benefit of a Circle is dramatically reduced if all the participants already view the topic the same way.
- Determine who will keep (facilitate) the Circle. If you are planning to be the keeper, recruit someone who will support you in the responsibility of maintaining a safe space for respectful dialogue.

- Choose a time and place for the talking Circle. Keep in mind the importance of a warm atmosphere, hospitality, and access. Make sure the space allows for a sufficient number of chairs to be arranged in a circle with no furniture inside the circle. Be mindful of possible time or calendar conflicts for particular interest groups.
- Extend invitations to those who may want to attend. Include some explanation of the topic, the purpose of the Circle, and the nature of the process. Personal invitations are the best way to generate participation. If you use a public notice, you might request that people send an RSVP. While the size of a talking Circle might comfortably be as large as twenty or thirty people, working with a larger group successfully will require additional planning and preparation. Circles of this nature have, in fact, been as large as a hundred.
- If the Circle turns out to be very large, keepers might suggest an additional guideline for participants to share responsibility in managing the time, so that everyone has a chance to speak. As part of emphasizing the need for brevity, they can even estimate the amount of time each person would have to speak, so that everyone could contribute and the Circle could still conclude as close to the ending time as possible. Naturally, some people may choose to pass and not to speak at all, which adds flexibility to the time limits.
- Choose a talking piece that will have meaning to the group and that will encourage respectful speaking and listening. Items from the natural environment, such as a stone, a shell, or a piece of wood, make wonderful talking pieces. Something with local significance, such as a carving or a community symbol, can be effective too, especially if it is connected to the issue. And then, of course, something playful or fun, like a stuffed animal or toy tractor, can help to lighten, relax, and humanize the atmosphere.
- Plan an opening ceremony that will set the tone for the Circle's space. A reading, some music, sharing images or photographs, or even a moment of silence can serve to

In this planning Circle, photos of the community provided the centerpiece, which is customarily arranged on the floor in the center of the circle of participants.

open a Circle. On one occasion, we brought photographs of important community assets. Then we asked participants to select a photo and comment on their personal relationship to that shared asset. In arranging these supportive elements of Circles—the ceremonies, the talking piece, and the centerpiece—be sure to choose things that are comfortable for you to use, but also make sure that they are not things that might be misunderstood, offensive, or alienating to others. The main point of the opening ceremony is to help the participants transition from their normal routine to the more intentional space of Circle dialogue.

- Decide whether you wish to create a centerpiece for the Circle. It can be very simple, such as a cloth with a candle and several talking piece options on it. Since the center-piece is the visual focal point for the Circle, planners can be creative about using it to focus on planning issues. We have placed in the center a collage of aerial photographs of the area, the mission statement of an organization, or a community plan. We have also used objects that have meaning related to the topic, such as a bowl of water when the Circle was about discussing water quality.

- Decide whether you will have food at the Circle and make the necessary arrangements. Food has a way of relaxing people and helping to build relationships. It can be shared at the beginning or the end of a Circle.

- Draft questions for the rounds of the Circle (stage 3). The questions that the keeper(s) poses to begin a round of the talking piece help participants to get acquainted and to engage the topic of dialogue.
- Find some quiet time to clear your mind and center yourself. Reflect on your intentions for the Circle. Focus on entering the Circle with openness and a heartfelt acceptance of others.

Stage 3: Convening the Circle

Having made the preparations, the keepers need to arrive early at the space. Make sure that the physical setup is appropriate. Set up the center if you have one planned. Take some time to breathe deeply and clear your mind of distractions. Then follow these steps to convene the Circle:

- Greet the participants as they arrive.
- When everyone is present and it is time to start, invite everyone to take a seat.
- Welcome participants and thank them for coming.
- Conduct the opening ceremony.
- Share again the purpose of the talking Circle and your intent.
- Introduce the talking piece and explain how it functions. Explain that the talking piece will be passed around the Circle to allow everyone an opportunity to speak. Only the person holding the talking piece may speak. The only exception is that the keeper (facilitator) may speak without the talking piece, if necessary, to maintain the healthy functioning of the Circle. Emphasize that a participant may choose not to speak by passing the talking piece or by holding it for a short time to introduce a moment of silence.
- For a first round of the talking piece, invite the participants to identify the values that they would like to have as a foundation for the dialogue. The group is likely to identify

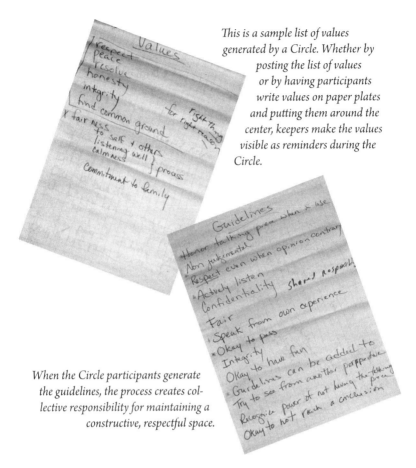

This is a sample list of values generated by a Circle. Whether by posting the list of values or by having participants write values on paper plates and putting them around the center, keepers make the values visible as reminders during the Circle.

When the Circle participants generate the guidelines, the process creates collective responsibility for maintaining a constructive, respectful space.

key words, such as honesty, respect, listening, openness, trust, or compassion. Invite the participants to write these values on paper plates and to place them around the center of the Circle.

- Explain the importance of developing guidelines that will help people align themselves with these values. For example, confidentiality as a guideline will support the values of honesty, respect, and trust. Describe the importance of the Circle as a place where people can speak their truths. Then pass the talking piece around the Circle again and ask participants to identify commitments they would like from the other participants that would help to make the Circle a place where they could speak their truth.

- Record the suggested guidelines on a flip chart or notepad. At the end of the round, read the list to the group. Ask the group whether they can commit to these guidelines for their process. Pass the talking piece again for individuals to respond. If there is not consensus, work to modify the guidelines, so that everyone can accept them.

- If there are time parameters for the Circle, explain what they are. As with very large Circles, ask the participants to keep these in mind and to take responsibility for making sure that everyone has an opportunity to speak. If it would save time to generate the guidelines in a brainstorming format, this is an option as well. As important as practical concerns about time are, though, experienced keepers tend to be cautious about intervening too quickly on someone speaking in the Circle. Keepers do not have a typical facilitation role. Rounds in Circles seem to have their own rhythm. Moreover, when keepers allow space for Circle members to deal with these issues themselves, participants become less dependent on the keeper to handle everything and increasingly step into their role as co-keeping Circle members. This naturally builds community.

These steps lay the foundation for the talking Circle process. Unless they already know each other, participants become involved in the Circle dialogue before they know who everyone is or why they are present. This is intentional. It allows people to interact without making assumptions based on titles or labels—their professional or community roles and their reasons for attending.

- Next, using the talking piece, initiate a round of introductions, even if the participants already know one another. Pose a question for participants to answer in addition to saying who they are. This question is intended to help people know more about each other before they begin to discuss the topic.

You might ask participants: How long have you been part of this community? What does this community mean to you? What life experience made you interested in this topic? What experience have you had talking about difficult or controversial subjects? One purpose of this question is to help participants see what they have in common, even though they may hold very different opinions on the topic. In this round, the keeper speaks first and models the kind of sharing that he or she is inviting from the participants.

After the round of introductions, participants are ready to engage the issue at hand. Before each round, the keeper poses a question to get the dialogue going. When the keeper receives the talking piece, he or she speaks as an equal participant. After each round, the keeper makes some summary comments that then lead into a question for the next round. The keeper's job at this stage, then, includes the following:

- Begin the dialogue about the main topic with a question that invites participants to share their thoughts and feelings about the issue. Pose the question for the group, and then pass the talking piece for responses. In this round, it is usually best for the keeper to speak last.
- Pass the talking piece again for people to respond to what they have heard from others in the previous round.
- If there is time for additional passes of the talking piece, frame questions that follow the major threads of dialogue that emerged in the earlier rounds.
- If people lapse into conventional discussion habits—if, for example, they interrupt, speak without the talking piece, or are disrespectful in any way—suspend the dialogue about the issue and revisit the guidelines. Ask participants if they can recommit to the guidelines or if any changes are needed.
- If the situation calls for it, identify steps that need to be taken after the Circle. Agree on who will do what, how things will be done, and who will follow up to support these activities.

- About ten to fifteen minutes before the ending time of the Circle, pass the talking piece again to close the dialogue in a good way. Ask participants how they feel about the experience of the Circle or invite them to make any closing comments. Let them know how much time is left and encourage them to pace their comments accordingly. If the group is large, help them do the math. For twenty participants to comment in the space of ten minutes, for example, each person has about half a minute to speak.
- Offer closing remarks that summarize the experience from your perspective. For example, identify what has been expressed relative to the Circle's original purpose; describe what you have learned; and honor the achievement of the group in creating and maintaining a respectful space. Thank everyone for his or her participation and commitment to a respectful process.
- Conduct a closing that marks the end of the process. A good closing ceremony reminds people of their interconnectedness and emphasizes the positive potentials in a situation. A short inspirational reading, a quote that honors the presence and contributions of the group, a few sentences that relate to the topic discussed, some music, or a few moments of silent reflection: these are all good ways to close a Circle.

  We would like to share a sample closing. This quote is attributed to Harry Houdini (1874–1926), the famous Jewish, Hungarian-American escape artist and skeptic:

  > Every being has a song. It's part of a web of sound and light that keeps this planet whole and functioning. Whales, trees, and humans have a song. When humans come fully into their hearts, the Earth will begin to function as a primary heart center in the universe. When we are loving, compassionate, trusting, and respectful, we are singing a song. It may not be heard by human ears, but it's a harmonic that makes this planet function.

Stage 4: Follow-Up

In a planning process, the follow-up that is needed after a talking Circle will vary, depending on the Circle's purpose. For example, if the Circle's intent is to provide input for a larger planning process, then the follow-up would be to take a summary of the talking Circle to the next stage of planning. This summary should also be available to everyone who attended the Circle. Another part of follow-up involves giving participants a way to keep track of the plan as it develops. Whatever follow-up is needed, it is critical to work out what needs to be done and who will do it before the Circle ends.

As a keeper, you may wish to seek feedback from participants about what did and did not work for them in the process. After the Circle, reflecting personally on your role as a keeper helps to develop your skills. Debriefing with your co-keeper or support person refines your abilities as a team. For those who use Circles regularly, Circles become a source of ongoing learning.

❧

These steps are provided as a general guide. Circles are not rigid. However, certain elements are essential: the opening and closing ceremonies, the use of the talking piece, and the creation of guidelines. With minor changes, these same steps can be used for celebration Circles, community-building Circles, or other Circles that serve a simple and straightforward purpose.

Conflict Circles and decision-making Circles are extremely useful for planning as well. But again, it is critical that keepers of these types of Circles have adequate Circle training. The Circle process offers a number of ways to deal with the complexity and emotional intensity that these purposes involve.

CHAPTER EIGHT

It All Ends Up in the Lake:
A Conflict over Water Quality

We would like to share one of our own experiences in Ontario, Canada. We wanted to introduce Circles to address a conflict about water quality at a municipal level, so we invited Kay to hold a Circle training and to mentor us through the process. This is our story.

For several years in the Bluewater area along Lake Huron's southern shoreline, water quality has been a hot issue. Everyone from the local communities to the national media has gotten caught up in the debate. Lakeshore residents accused the farmers of polluting the waterways that led to Lake Huron. They objected to the agricultural practices of spreading manure and spraying pesticides. In turn, the farm community blamed the lakeshore residents for faulty septic systems and towns for installing sewage bypasses. The lakeshore residents did not relate to the farmers, while the farmers did not relate to the lakeshore residents. The two communities were divided. Each had very little understanding of the other. Unable to communicate with each other, both sides began to threaten lawsuits. The rhetoric grew more strident. With no formal mechanism for dialogue in place, few could see any potential for arriving at a positive outcome.

Recognizing that we needed to find a way to address this conflict, we initiated a project to introduce Circles. From what we had learned, Circles create a space for dialogue between people who might not otherwise interact constructively. It was a risk. No one in our area had ever heard of Circles. Even so, the process offered something different from the usual facilitated mediation processes, of which most people were now cynical.

We needed to establish rapport and get into dialogue with community groups. So we discussed the Circle process at meetings with the local Federation of Agriculture, the local municipality, and the

Lakeshore residents, farmers, and planners came together through the Circle process seeking to work out their differences in a good way.

cottage associations. Although people were hesitant, they nonetheless lent their support and agreed to send volunteers to participate in a Circle training.

We arranged for an outside Circle trainer, Kay Pranis, to come in and train volunteer community members from both sides—the lakeshore residents and the agricultural communities. We also invited staff from various levels of government and other agencies to participate in the training. We believed that it was important for the community to be self-sustaining in its use of Circles. And we wanted the Circles to be led by local community members and not by outside "experts." We hoped that some of those who received the training would volunteer to organize Circles in their own communities and would agree to "co-keep" them, which they did.

Following the training, we held four Circles: two with rural and agricultural residents, and two with lakeshore residents. Holding separate Circles allowed each group to explore their own perceptions and views of their communities and their relationships to water. In these initial Circles, the participants did not need to justify or defend themselves. In each Circle of five to ten people, participants identified their concerns about water quality in their community. Then they compiled lists of their concerns on flip charts.

In a second set of Circles, these lists were exchanged with the lists made by the Circle of the opposing group. At these Circles, we asked each group about their reactions to the other group's list. Did anything on the list surprise them? Because these Circles were held separately, each group was able to experience the diversity of perspectives within their own group. They realized that not all of them were of the same mind. This realization helped to diffuse the tendency to speak in terms of "us" and "them." It also broke down the notion that "we" all have one view, and "they" all have another. By exchanging lists, the participants were able, still within the "safety" of their own groups, to acknowledge some of the concerns that both groups had. They also began to challenge perceptions they may have had about the other group's concerns as well as to expand their knowledge of the "other."

After we held these separate Circles for the opposing groups, we organized a combined Circle. The purpose of this Circle was to bring together people from both communities to explore and understand the issues more fully. The purpose was not to try to resolve the issue. Everyone had real concerns and trepidation before the meeting. We wondered who would show up and how people would interact. The two keepers—volunteers from each community—were nervous about their roles. Could they hold the space for people who had become so polarized to express their strong views and potentially intense emotions? They knew people were coming who would normally dominate the airtime, while others would be there who never spoke up in meetings. Their great and only hope was that the Circle process would manage this and generate a different experience for everyone.

That evening, about twenty-five people showed up. We all had dinner together. Then we gathered in a Circle without tables in front of us. Although each of the separate groups had previously discussed their values and guidelines, we went through these exercises again as a combined group. This was very important. Everyone needed to agree on the basic assumptions that would guide the discussion. They had to know where they could turn if things went awry.

In this case, the process began by holding separate Circles for the opposing interest groups. When the two groups came together in a Circle later on, the separate guidelines generated by the two different groups were brought to the combined Circle. The larger Circle then came to a consensus on a combined list of guidelines.

By the end of the evening, to everyone's surprise and relief, the Circle process had met the challenge. People had experienced an in-depth and passionate conversation. They had expressed extremely divergent opinions on issues that had divided their communities. But because of the Circle process, everything was expressed respectfully and "in a good way." One person said,

> I can't help but reflect on how different this meeting was from other meetings that I've attended. Each of us took a turn talking about the issue. . . . I think we all felt comfortable. I felt as if others were listening, and I wasn't being judged. I found myself sharing my deep concerns on what has been a very difficult issue.

Everyone left genuinely surprised by what they had just experienced. They looked forward to more Circle dialogues in the future. The process gave them hope in who they could be together, in spite of how divided they had been. And it gave them hope in the possibility of coming to some positive resolution down the road if they continued with the process. They were not there yet by any means, but at least

Feed lots raise a number of issues for communities: smell, pollution, manure. Feed lots have been very controversial and have generated highly polarized and bitter disputes. The intensity of these disputes creates a difficult challenge for planners.

they had a vision of how they might get there, which was something they did not have before.

The next week, we received a phone call from one of the keepers. Just a few days after this Circle, a local farm had a major manure spill. Should we organize a Circle to deal with this? Over the next few days, we discussed this option along with the legalities raised by the spill. The Ministry of Environment was moving toward legal action. We were concerned about the legalities of people speaking to the issue when court action was pending. Also, we didn't know whether we had the experience or the confidence to take on this issue with the community. In view of our professional roles as planners, we decided not to get directly involved. However, we told the community volunteer keepers that they had our personal support if they decided to go ahead. In the end, no one called a Circle. The legal proceedings went forward. And the community ended up being further polarized as a result.

A year later, we were able to invite Kay back and to bring together some of the people who had originally been trained. We asked them to reflect on their experiences with the Circle process since the training. We wanted to hear both their impressions of the process and the ways they had used Circles in their own contexts since. This Circle gathering gave us much insight.

Some people felt a sense of disappointment that we had not been able to hold a Circle around the manure spill issue. They were concerned that some of the goodwill and communication that had developed in the previous Circles may have been lost. Others expressed a commitment to keep trying to use the Circle process, even in other areas of their lives. Still others observed that more constructive conversations were now occurring about the water quality issue than there otherwise would have been. One woman said, "I saw that, at the root of a lot of issues of water quality, there was a real difference in how rural people view the world and how urban people view the world."

The possibility of using Circles to talk about these issues remains. As one person stated, "We don't see things in the same way, and we need to talk about why we don't." Many people shared the realization that the Circle is an ongoing process that is never finished. The conversations that we need to have with each other and that matter most are conversations that must continue over a long, long time.

❧

This use of the Circle process did not bring a tidy resolution to a deeply rooted, complex, community conflict. Instead, it opened a space for dialogues to continue on many different levels. And while that space, which opened so significantly, may seem to have narrowed soon after, the follow-up Circle with the trained volunteers showed how much the attitudes in the community had changed. The Circles had created the potential for further conversations. The experience brought a shift in how the two sides saw each other. Community members now knew how to bring people together step-by-step from both sides of the issue. And they knew they could use this tool for other concerns and in other areas of their lives as well. Their reflections and responses a year later indicate that they had experienced the power of Circle. It had changed them and their community, and they wanted to keep using Circles as an important part of their lives.

 CHAPTER NINE

Exploring the Possibilities: The Potentials for Using Circles in Planning

Circles can serve planning practices in two important and yet distinct ways. First, the Circle process offers an innovative way to engage the community. Circles can build trust across deep divisions. And they build communities. Because everyone takes part in the decision-making process, everyone shares in the responsibility for how things go.

Second, the Circle process invites planners to think about the public and their role in planning quite differently. Some aspects of Circles can contribute to the more conventional approaches. But on a deeper level, Circles promote a philosophical shift in how we approach our work. Planners come to view communities in a very different way. As a result, we interact with the public—those we serve—differently.

Using Circles is not, though, a question of all or nothing. Even one or two components of the Circle process can deepen the dialogue in more traditional contexts and can bring a number of benefits. In this chapter, we explain how planners can use the Circle process either in its full application or by borrowing some of its elements. We also explore how both these approaches can enhance some of the conventional methods that planners use to engage the public.

The Spectrum of Circles That Planners Can Use

Planners draw on many techniques to engage the public. Legislative requirements, logistics, politics, personal preferences, circumstances: these are some of the factors we consider when we choose a method for bringing the public into the planning process. In all instances, planners should look for a tool or approach they believe will be most effective and appropriate for the specific need or situation. By and large, planners are on board with this goal. We want to provide meaningful ways for the public to take part in making the decisions that will affect us all, perhaps for generations. This just makes sense, because it makes for better, more satisfying outcomes all around. The Circle process is one technique that planners have not widely explored, but it holds the promise of bringing many benefits—some quite profound.

In chapter 5, we described some different types of Circles and explained how they varied according to the reasons for their use. The fact that Circles are so flexible and powerful allows for these and many other uses. Figure 9.1 presents eleven different types of Circles. Seven of them have clear applications in planning. The other four are less likely to be used in planning contexts.

This figure also organizes the types of Circles along a spectrum of intensity and complexity. Those with greater intensity and complexity call for facilitators who have more training and experience, because the potential for conflict is greater. The training is not about giving the keepers better skills as mediators. Rather, its goal is to help them understand how the Circle process itself resolves conflicts. Essentially, keepers learn how to trust the Circle and hence how *not* to step in as personal mediators.

The types of Circles that we describe as being less intense and complex deal with more routine issues. These Circles are not aimed at confronting the unpredictable, resolving conflicts, or working toward a consensus decision. The dynamics in these Circles are more straightforward, and the emotions involved are usually less challenging. Although Circle training always helps, the keepers of these Circles do not need to be formally trained.

As a result, planners can easily facilitate these types of Circles without any formal Circle training. Naturally, they need to be grounded in the core elements of Circles, such as using a talking piece, discussing values, and coming to an agreement on guidelines. But with these basics, planners can soon discover all sorts of ways of using Circles and of integrating the process into their professional practice. Yes, there will be challenges and things to watch out for, as we discuss in chapter 12. But if planners start with the simpler uses, an understanding of how Circles work can grow in a natural way. Confidence in

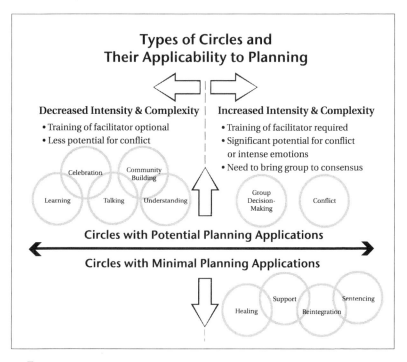

Figure 9.1

the process will build, and this will lay a good foundation for using Circles in more challenging situations.

Less Intense or Complex Circles

Circles that are likely to be less intense and complex include Circles of celebration, talking, community building, learning, and understanding. We describe these Circles as being distinct, and yet their purposes often overlap. A Circle held for one reason can end up fulfilling a number of objectives. Here are some examples of how each type of Circle can be used in planning.

Celebration or Honoring Circles. Celebration Circles are by far the easiest to use. A planning office might hold a Circle to celebrate a

Learning Circles empower participants to work from a shared base of information.

personal achievement, someone's retirement, or the receipt of an award. Planners might also use a Circle to celebrate a community's accomplishments. In Oregon, for example, after building some homes for families with low incomes, Habitat for Humanity volunteers and the families came together in a Circle to celebrate this achievement. Using the key to a home as a talking piece, people shared what the experience had meant to them.

Dialogue Circles. Dialogue Circles bring together diverse views and provide a safe space for people to share their thoughts and knowledge. The task of developing a neighborhood plan offers a prime example of how this type of Circle can be used. During the early stages of creating a plan for a community, planners invited residents to the homes of fellow community members to talk about planning issues in general. Many meetings were held throughout the community. As residents sat around the kitchen table or living room, they chatted about how their community had changed and shared their hopes for the future. These discussions helped residents connect with the planning process, confront its limits and potentials, and realize how much it affected their lives.

Learning Circles. Planning schools can use Circles to demonstrate how the process can work in a public context. Learning Circles can play an especially critical role in planning. When community members lack certain technical or specialized information, their lack of knowledge prevents them from fully engaging in the dialogue. Learning Circles help to level the playing field. Planners can use these Circles to give community members the information they need to participate effectively. For example, a planner may want to invite an environmental specialist in to teach the group some basics about the subject under discussion. Participants can then reflect on the new information and relate it to their own experiences. The Circle can also elicit the natural wisdom of the group.

Here is an example where a learning Circle would have been useful. In a rural community, a beef farmer was storing the solid manure from his cattle in piles covered with tarps on a vacant vegetable field next to several residential properties. The neighbors began to complain to the municipality about flies and odors. Community tensions escalated. The conflict was resolved only after an agricultural engineer was called in to review the situation. He explained that what the farmer was doing with the manure was appropriate; it was a legitimate approach to composting. A learning Circle would have offered the residents a greater understanding of the farming practice, and tensions could have been resolved much earlier.

Planner Randy French describes another experience of using the Circle process to facilitate learning:

> One experience I had with the Native community was facilitating a meeting between an Ojibway Elder and an environmental consulting firm. The consulting firm wanted to learn more about the Native culture. Through the Circle process, the Elder was able to address all of their questions. This group included about thirty to forty people, so it was on the larger side for a Circle. But by the time it was finished, all of the questions had been answered.

Learning Circles are also used in public planning courses to help students digest the material and to experience the process firsthand. Dialogue Circles and learning Circles are quite similar. Learning Circles simply have a more defined agenda. In learning Circles, students go into subjects more deeply and are more inclined to integrate the new knowledge with their lives. In planning contexts, learning Circles might also be used after a guest speaker's presentation to help the group integrate what was said.

Community-Building Circles. These Circles have any number of applications in planning. For example, two groups came together in a Circle to evaluate the success of an environmental project. Because funding was an ongoing challenge, they also wanted to figure out their next steps with the project. Although the two groups had very different orientations, the Circle enabled them to explore options and potential directions for their work. To start off, they reached a consensus about the project's success and its effectiveness to date. Then the group went on to identify a number of practical solutions for how to keep the project going. In this case, the Circle allowed participants to share information and to generate ideas for revamping the program. More than that, though, they experienced what it was like to bridge differences in a common effort. Their sense of community expanded through the Circle experience.

Circles of Understanding. Circles can play a huge role in helping us understand each other. People speak with a candor and authenticity in Circles that rarely happens in other public or even private spaces. In one case, for example, farmers and cottagers met as a community to talk about some of the environmental issues that they shared. A few of the lakeshore residents had Circle experience, so they suggested that the group establish an ongoing talking Circle to explore some of the more critical farm issues. In particular, they wanted to discuss how livestock manure was handled and processed on farm fields and how these practices affected the environment. Their request followed a spill of manure that led to a fish kill. When they proposed to hold the Circles, the cottager group also made an unexpected offer to work with the farm community to help them get more support from the government. From a place of understanding that the Circles had made possible, the groups began to work together to meet the needs that people had on all sides.

More Intense or Complex Circles

As we've explained, some of the reasons for holding Circles involve higher levels of intensity and complexity, both in emotions and in the nature of the issue. These Circles might address an outright conflict, or they might look at the tensions that could be leading to conflicts. In such cases, emotions are intense. Standoffs between people can surface at any time, and the issues afford no easy solutions. Facilitating a difficult conversation in any kind of public process requires experience, and this is true for these types of Circles as well. Circle training helps facilitators understand how the process—and the philosophy behind it—can "hold the space" for addressing painful or difficult conflicts. With training, keepers do not have to reinvent how Circles can deal with such situations.

Planners face many situations where these Circles could help enormously. Two areas stand out: when conflicts need to be resolved, and when a group needs to make a decision.

Conflict Circles. Conflict is inherent in public planning. Conflicts over planning issues often end up in the courts or other tribunals. However, these formal ways of resolving conflicts usually produce win-lose outcomes; the underlying issues remain unresolved. One side walks away unhappy, maybe even smoldering for revenge. They often hope that what is decided will fail. Win-lose outcomes are not a good way to build communities or to promote good, long-term relations.

Mediation, negotiation, and Circles offer less formal ways of sorting out conflicts. These methods put building relationships at the center of the process. With this focus, the potentials for win-win outcomes and solutions that satisfy everyone go way up. Building relationships and getting at the roots of conflicts: these are key characteristics of the Circle process and why it is so powerful in resolving some of the most difficult conflicts. For example,

This former auto and truck factory, which was once a central organizing factor in defining the neighborhood, is closing. The community now faces many issues and hard decisions, from job loss to residual toxicity to what to do with highly valuable land. This raises the planning question: How does a community make such a complex decision with all the impacts and opportunities that go with it?

The community was torn apart over the issue. For decades, everyone assumed that the beach was public property. Cottage owners whose cottages did not sit directly on the beach used public walkways to pass by and enjoy the entire shoreline. But then a legal verdict ruled that the lakefront cottagers owned the beach to the high water mark and that they could deny access to the others. The ruling divided this once tranquil community. The province became involved and spent a half million dollars on lawyers and mediation to bring the parties together and find a solution. But it did not work. Such a situation is a perfect opportunity to use a Circle.

Group Decision-Making Circles. This may be the most complex— and perhaps the most resource-intensive—application of the Circle process in planning. However, it also has the greatest potential for helping planners achieve their highest goals. In 1969, Sherry Arnstein argued for redistributing decision-making power in the planning process. She argued that public planning has the best chances for success when it involves the citizens who will be affected. Citizens need a voice not only in the easy decisions but also in the complex and difficult choices that planners must make. Circles offer a means for such citizen participation.

Chapter 10 gives an example of how a planning group used Circles in the decision-making process to create a correctional facility based on First Nation values and ways. A community in Ontario, Canada, used Circles during the early stages of forming an official plan for their community. In another area, community members came together in Circles to develop an approach for consulting the public about their planning process.

Circles can also be used to develop large-scale planning proposals. Granted, Circles can be logistically challenging when many people are involved. Yet, even if organizers are not comfortable with using large Circles, Circles can still play a role in the process. They can create spaces for more detailed discussions in concurrent or complementary Circles. And they can be used to involve the community in decision-making at public meetings. Here is one example of how Circles are being used in creative and powerful ways.

Barry Stuart is a leader in the modern use of the Circle process. He has used many aspects of Circles in corporations and institutions as well as in addressing public- and private-sector issues. He is currently using Circles as an integral part of a multiparty process involving First Nations, Federal, Provincial, and Municipal governments, commercial harvesters, recreational interest groups, environmental NGOs [non-governmental organizations] and all other interested parties. The goal is to develop collaborative management approaches to the salmon fishery in British Columbia.

The challenges are both enormous and complex. The demand for salmon is increasing, while the supply is diminishing due to a myriad of problems, especially development and climate change. With so many livelihoods, lifestyles, constitutional rights, and historic practices at stake, intense emotions and strongly held views permeate the struggle to find a way that is sustainable for fish and people.

Meeting in Circle, participants have engaged many of the Circle values and its processes. Coming together in this way has

This community-based Circle initiative worked to strengthen their community by using the Circle process. It brought together people who would normally never come together. In the process, they created long-lasting relationships.

helped to create a safe place for the kind of dialogue needed to build consensus. These dialogues began with exploring how to have a conversation among very different interests. Participants then turned to designing a process for addressing the substantive issues they faced. By splitting into working groups focused on addressing specific critical issues, the group as a whole is coming up with genuinely new approaches. As confidence builds, the hope is that a consensus can be achieved that will change government processes, so that the planning and management of the salmon fisheries can be done collaboratively.

The process has built new relationships based on under-standing, trust, and mutual respect. Most importantly, parties are recognizing the need to work together. As innovative ideas emerge, they are gaining hope that, by working together, they may be able to resolve seemingly intractable problems.

Applying Elements of Circles to Other Planning Processes

Circles provide spaces for sharing stories and for building a base for diverse people to understand each other. Circles also promote a shift in how planners relate with citizens. This shift in the relationship between planners and communities changes the environment for everyone. People gain hope and encouragement from a growing sense of what might be possible when they come together in a good way. Instead of fearing differences or opposing views, participants come to understand how valuable these differences are in forming balanced, wise, and sustainable decisions.

Incorporating even a few elements of the Circle process can make a difference. Planners use all sorts of techniques in their roles as group facilitators, which they must do every day. Here are some of the circumstances where planners might consider using some of the Circle's elements:

- Facilitating or leading a discussion; conducting a brainstorming session; participating on a panel; or organizing a focus group: all these are great opportunities for using various elements of Circles. What planners are looking for are group processes that are flexible and that allow room for innovation.

- When planners contribute as experts in government-initiated public meetings, they can also engage elements of Circles. Though an elected official might chair the meeting, planners can still engage the audience in exploring values or discussing guidelines for how we want to approach the issue. Sometimes planners do not have much say in the overall approach to the meeting or dialogue, but they certainly can have an influence.

- Even when planners participate in a process that is determined by legislation or by some external agency, they can introduce some of the Circle's elements. In such cases, the planner's influence over the process is very limited. Nonetheless, they still have control over how they conduct themselves and how they engage with others in the meeting.

The more planners understand how Circles work, the more they will find ways to bring elements of Circles into their group processes. Using a talking piece, for example, gives each participant an equal voice. It also tells the group that those who are arranging the meeting are committed to hearing everyone's views. Contests for being heard or power plays are not what this process is about. Discussing values and guidelines creates a positive, constructive framework for governing a meeting. It also tells the group that the organizers are not going to control the outcome by how they manage the process. The group decides which values will provide the best means for arriving at a good result. Given this basis of shared values and guidelines, even in a regular meeting format, the group's members can be involved in holding each other to what they have decided.

These practices create a different group dynamic. Yet more than that, they send a message about the organizers' intentions. It shows that they are committed to using a fair process that involves the community. Using a Circle approach to any degree tells participants that the decision is not already made and that it is not going to be made in a top-down, autocratic way. It sends a powerful message of respect for citizen participation. And it shows a commitment to fair, egalitarian processes, even before the dialogue begins.

The key here is that planners become sufficiently familiar with Circles to use elements of them, even when it might not be possible to carry out the full process. Small changes, seemingly innocuous to skeptics, can have a big effect, more than what might be evident on the surface.

Beyond these observable elements, Circles embody a philosophy that is quite different from an adversarial, win-lose approach. Being inclusive and respectful of differences, listening and speaking from the heart, sharing personal experiences, and seeking consensus all reflect a philosophy, even a way of being. The intention to come from a Circle philosophy is, in itself, significant. And it can make a difference. The philosophy inspires us to respond to issues, conflicts, and each other from a more peacemaking perspective.

Knowing the benefits of Circles enables planners to bring them into their practice in any number of ways. Figure 9.2 shows the main elements of Circles that can be used in conjunction with conventional public processes. Some of these elements are more tangible than others.

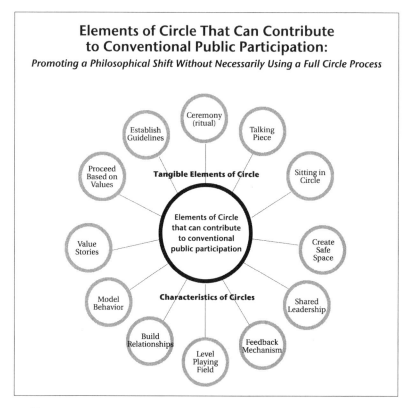

Figure 9.2

Using the Circle's Tangible Elements

Discussing values and guidelines; using a talking piece; opening and closing with ceremonies; and sitting in a circle: these are the more tangible elements of Circles that can be incorporated into other processes.

Values. Identifying shared values, such as honesty, respect, and fairness, grounds the dialogue in what the participants consider to be most important.

Guidelines. Guidelines, such as "Listen actively" and "Don't interrupt," serve to hold a group to higher standards of accountability.

Once established, these guidelines can be used by the group from one meeting to the next—or changed as needed.

Talking Piece. Again, using a talking piece makes a clear statement to participants that the organizers are committed to giving everyone an equal opportunity to speak. It also slows the pace of the discussion. A talking piece can be helpful in many meeting formats. The planner can also consciously incorporate aspects of the talking piece without actually using one. For example, planners can make sure that a meeting is facilitated or chaired in such a way that everyone has a chance to speak.

Ceremonies. A ceremony at the beginning of a meeting provides a transition between the stress and busyness of daily life and the discussion at hand. While the concept is foreign to many public processes, it is very effective in creating a more thoughtful approach to dialogue. For example, when we met with some farmers, we wanted to help the group move into a more reflective space. To do this, we brought a basket of various farm-related items—a small bag of fertilizer, a packet of topsoil, some seed corn, a toy tractor, and other things—and asked the farmers to pick one and talk about what it meant to them. Ceremonies invite us to step back and consider a bigger view, what we have in common, or what is most important in life. After a ceremony—which can be very simple—we are more inclined to approach a specific issue from a broader perspective.

Circle Seating. Sitting in a circle does much to establish an open and interactive dialogue. People can see each other, make eye contact, speak directly, and, as a result, be much more accountable to each other and the group.

We want to share three stories that illustrate how these tangible Circle elements can blend with other processes.

> *Two rural towns were locked in a nasty boundary dispute.*
> *Growth in one of the towns was constrained by its municipal*
> *boundaries. The town was literally out of space and could not*
> *accommodate any more new businesses or housing. The second*

rural town was equally constrained by the absence of water and sewer services, which the first town had. Most of the communication between the two municipalities was going on in the local newspaper. After many months of this kind of debate, the two towns realized that the process was going nowhere. They agreed to ask an impartial third party to help them with the process. A planner and an engineer were brought in to help them resolve the issue.

The process for resolving the boundary dispute was largely prescribed by three participants who were appointed from each town. They agreed that the planner and engineer would use a combination of fact-finding and facilitated negotiation to resolve the dispute. The planner's first response was to borrow from her knowledge of the Circle process. She first helped the parties in conflict identify the values that they wanted to bring to the group's process. Then she helped them use these values as a springboard for establishing guidelines for the process: How did the group want to conduct themselves and treat each other as they addressed the conflict?

The process eventually failed to come to a resolution for a variety of political reasons. Perhaps most significantly, the group could not overcome a basic lack of trust. Yet throughout the negotiations, one positive feature was that participants repeatedly referred to the guidelines that they had established for the group's conduct. Reflecting on the whole experience later, the planner couldn't help wondering what might have been possible if she had been able to use the full Circle process. Would this process have helped the two towns build the trust and mutual understanding they needed to resolve the boundary dispute?

❧

A planning organization at the state level gave outgoing council members exit surveys to comment on their experiences on the council. The members identified a number of concerns, both about board governance and about how council members had treated each other. In their experience, opinions had not always been heard; discussions had not always been respectful; and some folks had not had time to speak on an issue. At their inaugural meeting, the new council responded by spending time reflecting on their values and developing guidelines for how to be with each other in meetings. In an amazingly quick process, the council agreed on the following list of guidelines. They also committed to reviewing these guidelines at the start of each council meeting and printed them on the back of everyone's "name tent" (the folded card placed in front of people with their name on it).

- Come to meetings prepared.
- Focus on the "big picture."
- Bring your ideas, not your agendas.
- Listen to and value all opinions.
- Speak up on matters of importance.
- Be honest.
- Be courteous and respectful.
- Be empathetic and consider others' perspectives.
- Be objective, focus on the issue; put your personal feelings aside.
- Be solution-oriented and move forward.
- Support your volunteer colleagues, and respect their role on the council.

❧

UNHABITAT invited us to facilitate a meeting at a major international gathering on "Sustainable Relief and Reconstruction." Given the time we had for the discussion (1.5 hours), we decided to use a conventional style of facilitation. However, we also drew on some of the lessons we had learned from Circles.

We arrived at the meeting room well in advance. But, as so often happens at conferences, the previous session was running overtime. When the doors finally opened and the room emptied, we rushed in to rearrange the seating. Some people suggested that, in the interest of time, we should simply proceed with the existing layout—rows of chairs. But people chipped in, and we were able to set up concentric circles to accommodate the sixty to seventy international participants who flooded in. It did not take long to do this. Sitting among the participants were a number of experts, each of whom had prepared position papers.

Already, choosing a circle layout and engaging the group in creating the space set a collaborative, positive tone. It almost served the role of a ceremony, because people could see that something different was going to happen in this space from the usual lecturer–audience format.

As we began our discussions, we observed right away what a difference it made for all of us to be sitting in circles. Of course, the experts brought much depth to the discussion. However, their placement among the other participants as part of the circles changed the group's dynamics. The experts were seen as part of the group and not set apart from the attendees. This helped to facilitate a free-flowing discussion. Moreover, participants could be in eye contact with each other. In this international gathering, nonverbal communication contributed significantly to the richness of the dialogue. The group engaged in an easy, respectful exchange of information, and many participants shared comments and stories.

Some people described it as the best session at the conference. It certainly created a constructive space for sharing information and pondering what the best next steps might be.

As facilitators, we recognized that the success of the session was due in large part to our use of some of the Circle's elements. It clearly changed the dynamics. What would have otherwise been a standard, non-participatory, one-way information download became a genuine exchange of ideas, knowledge, and experiences.

~

Using the Circle's Intangible Elements

Circles have a number of less tangible characteristics, and these features support a philosophical shift in how planners interact with groups as well. In the full Circle process, these intangible qualities develop naturally from the use of the Circle's more tangible elements.

However, there are times when we just cannot pass a talking piece, sit in a circle, or discuss values and guidelines. Yet even then, we can still call on these less tangible features and see their benefits to the dialogue. These less visible features suggest that "being in Circle" is not something that is, at its core, physical or outward; it is a mind-set.

Tours and group activities, such as this tour of the county's watershed, can strengthen relationships, which is essential to the Circle process. This is a case of applying Circle principles and values without actually sitting in a Circle. Planners often draw on traditional planning techniques, such as this one, in combination with the Circle process and the principles and values underlying it.

By intentionally designing public processes with a Circle mind-set, planners can begin to tap the Circle's potential to deepen even conventional public processes.

Here are some of the Circle's more intangible elements that can be used to convey or "seed" a Circle mind-set.

Valuing Stories. Stories are an integral part of Circles. Conventional planning approaches, however, tend not to value or make use of them. They are nice but irrelevant to the job at hand. A Circle mind-set takes a different view. Personal stories bring out the values, beliefs, and sense of meaning in events and life experiences. Providing spaces for people to share their stories and for others to respect the importance of what they share is critical to building understanding. Stories help us understand both the people and the issues on much deeper levels. Randy French writes about his experience

In my work with developing "lake plans," one of the questions I pose to Circle participants is to ask them to share their memories of the lake. Sharing these memories with the group helps to make the Circle interact better—it breaks down barriers to communication.

Safe Space. Most of us like to feel comfortable and secure, and this is especially true when we are discussing highly contentious issues. Whether we feel safe or not has to do with both the physical environment and the emotional atmosphere. Arranging for a neutral space to meet, providing appropriate introductions, welcoming people, and sharing food can all contribute to a positive meeting. They meet the basic physical concerns. As for the emotional side, discussing values and agreeing on guidelines assures people that they can express their point of view without being attacked or run down in some way.

Model Behavior. Principles of respect and inclusivity are central to how Circles function. One of the ways that keepers play a role in upholding these principles is by modeling behavior that reflects them. Keepers demonstrate how to treat others in respectful and inclusive ways by how they conduct themselves. Yet facilitators do not need to be in a Circle to do this. They can model principled behavior in other meeting formats as well. Through their own personal conduct, they can help set a standard.

Shared Leadership. In Circles, leadership is shared among all the participants. This important lesson can be incorporated into other processes. Community members can be encouraged to actively participate in the dialogue. But more than that, they can help lead the process and share responsibility for how it goes. Sharing in the leadership increases everyone's sense of ownership. Shared leadership also opens the process to a diversity of opinions. Down the road, it makes it much easier for planners to implement the community's chosen direction. People are on board with the plan because they played a significant role in making the decision.

Honest Feedback Mechanisms. Circles provide participants and the keeper with immediate and ongoing feedback. Here again, this enables participants to take ownership of the process, because they can monitor each other's ideas, concerns, and interests as they arise. Creating channels for open and honest feedback always improves a group process. It creates transparency, so that everyone knows what the issues are and who is saying what about them. In non-Circle formats, it can be challenging to do this effectively. Even so, planners can take steps in this direction. They can hand out evaluation forms after meetings. They can also work to establish an open environment that encourages feedback throughout the meeting.

Level the Playing Field. One of the most basic concepts of Circles is that all the participants are treated equally. Each person has an equal opportunity to speak, and each opinion is valued. Barriers between people—such as position, rank, job, or affiliations—are minimized. This valuable concept can serve as a goal in other public processes. Planners can strive to ensure that as many voices as possible are heard, valued, and integrated into planning discussions and policies.

Building Relationships. Perhaps the most important aspect of Circles is their focus on relationships. As we explained in chapter 3, the Circle process has us spend as much time on getting acquainted and developing an understanding of each other as we spend on discussing the issues and planning actions. For some, this focus on cultivating relationships seems counterproductive. It takes time, and for folks who are focused on projects or concerned about schedules, it can seem like a waste of time.

But in practice, just the opposite is the case. From a basis of good relationships, work can get done with much greater ease and efficiency. How a group functions; the quality of the decisions it makes; how those decisions are eventually implemented: all these critical aspects are greatly improved when people can establish good relationships up front.

In conventional group processes, planners will have to work with the situation at hand to see where and how relationship-building can fit in. But even something as simple as taking time for introductions or having snacks available at the beginning, during breaks, and at the end of a meeting can help. Food has a way of promoting informal, friendly conversation. A more elaborate strategy to build relationships might be to plan a bus trip that brings together a number of interested parties. As planners recognize how important good relationships are to the success of their work, all sorts of creative ways to strengthen them will emerge.

∾

A planning department set a goal to bring diverse interests from the community together to develop a plan for a sustainable way of life. To start off, a number of agency and community representatives came together to discuss how to draw each of their sectors into the process. Those who were invited were all influential people. Over the lunch hour, the program included a "Sustainability Scavenger Hunt." This served two purposes. It focused people on the topic at hand. But it also contributed to building relationships. It gave folks a chance to work together, which they would later need to do to engage the wider community, develop the plan, and facilitate its implementation.

 CHAPTER TEN

Planning the Healing Lodge

JANE MILLER-ASHTON'S EXPERIENCE

Jane Miller-Ashton of Correctional Service Canada (CSC) shared with us this story of the use of Circles to plan a special prison for federally sentenced First Nations1 women in Canada. The story reflects her perspective on that experience, since Jane was deeply involved in the process by representing CSC.

In 1989, the Canadian government created a federal task force to improve the conditions for women who were serving federal prison sentences in Canada. This task force formed a working partnership between the government, the Canadian Elizabeth Fry Society,[2] and representatives of First Nations women's organizations. Each of these three groups held widely divergent worldviews and approached things in very different ways. The First Nations women played a key role on the task force because First Nations people are sent to prison at far higher rates than other populations. The process turned out to be quite challenging. The CSC, a government agency, was not accustomed to working in such an equal partnership with non-government groups. Neither was it used to giving them such a significant role in decision-making.

From the start, the task force struggled with the clash of histories and cultures. One of the First Nations women suggested that an Elder could help with the process and with ways to understand the cultural realities of First Nations. So a First Nations Elder joined the task force, and she began sharing teachings about First Nations' ways of life. She explained some of the teachings of the Medicine Wheel and how First Nations people come together to work things out.

With her support, the task force was able to build consensus about closing the old prison. They also agreed on decentralizing the women's prison population by building a Healing Lodge as an option for federally sentenced First Nations women, as well as four other regional prisons for women serving federal sentences. The Healing Lodge would operate according to the teachings and cultural practices of First Nations people.

With unusual speed, the government accepted these recommendations. A National Implementation Committee was set up with Jane carrying the responsibility for the CSC's role in the process. A second group was created to work specifically on planning the Healing Lodge for federally sentenced First Nations women. The members were primarily non-governmental First Nations women as well as some government representatives. Eventually, the group included three Elders to support the process. From the beginning, following First Nations teachings, the group used the Circle process as the best way to work together. This group became known as the "Healing Lodge Planning Circle." Jane was part of this group as well.

The Healing Lodge Planning Circle developed criteria for where to locate the facility. After reviewing many possible sites, the Circle recommended a location. The group then designed a vision for the Healing Lodge and created a plan of operation to go with it. This plan included the facility's physical structure, its programming for the women, and the mechanisms for security and control.

Led by the Elders, the group used many different layers of Circles for every aspect of the planning process. They used talking Circles to discuss content issues. They held healing Circles when the process brought up painful memories or experiences. And they used teaching Circles when the group got stuck and needed to reconnect with core values and principles. The Elders also used Circle ceremonies to help members access their deep selves and stay in service to their shared vision.

Sometimes the group got locked in disagreements. The Elders would then have everyone assemble at the end of the long meeting room or somewhere apart from the normal working area. As the group stood in a circle, the Elders did a smudging ceremony. They burned ceremonial plants and washed the smoke over each person. This served to clear away any negative energy and to cleanse each person. After the smudging, the Elders asked each person to express why he or she was involved in the process. This inevitably brought people back to the shared vision of a Healing Lodge for federally sentenced First Nations women. The power and energy of the shared vision gave the group the will to keep working together. Despite different perspectives and difficult topics, the group persisted in finding common ground, and this helped them to keep moving toward the shared vision.

This overall picture describes the planning project and the key role that Circles had in the process. It is hard to depict all the ways that the Circle guided the group and made a good outcome possible. A few specific situations that the group faced illustrate the nature and operations of Circles—methods that were certainly different from standard CSC procedures.

For example, when the group was working on choosing a site, the Circle took into account the concerns of both the First Nations people and the government (Corrections). Being a collaborative process, the Circle developed criteria for the site that included both First Nations and Correctional considerations. The First Nations' criteria called for plenty of land around the facility and for a stream or river—some form of running water—on the land. The major concern for Corrections was, of course, security. The planning Circle examined all the applications from communities to build the lodge in their area. Then the Circle used a decision-making process that enabled the group to choose a location by consensus. By the time the final decision was made, everyone was on board with the choice.

With a site chosen, the Healing Lodge Planning Circle was ready to design the building as well as the program and its operations. But a question arose about who could participate at the local level. Could people from the community be involved in the planning process? Following the principles of the Circle, the Elders suggested that it should be open to anyone who wished to come. Jane, the primary CSC organizer, and her colleagues were worried at first that several hundred people might show up and want to take part. But the group reached consensus on this issue, too, and agreed with the Elders. The process had to be open to anyone who wanted to have a voice. Including community members turned out to be a very wise choice. Some of the local people were indeed worried that having a prison in their community would negatively affect the area.

So the Planning Circle made a public invitation. Anyone in the

First Nations reserve where the Healing Lodge was going to be built as well as anyone in the nearby town were invited to be part of the planning group. Around two hundred people did come to the first gathering. The Elders used the Circle process and a talking piece, so that each person had an opportunity to speak and have input. As the gatherings continued over time, the numbers of people who showed up dwindled. People felt they had been heard, and they trusted that the core members had their interests at heart.

The size of the Planning Circle eventually settled down to about twenty members. This number included some non–First Nations local community people as well as members from the reserve that had been chosen as the site for the facility. From time to time, new members joined to provide expertise, such as government and public works people, architects, or builders. All the consultants received the Elders' teachings and were included as part of the talking and healing Circles that made up the planning process. Each decision was made by consensus.

Throughout the process, the group took whatever time was needed for ceremony, for talking Circles that allowed everyone to speak, and for healing Circles that took care of the group's emotional and personal needs. Especially at the beginning, when Jane reported back to CSC headquarters, she often could not provide a standard progress report. CSC people began to be apprehensive about the use of an unconventional approach because of the time the group needed to spend in Circles building consensus. Would the Healing Lodge actually get built? Would its construction be severely delayed? Would the group be stuck in process and not be able to make decisions or get things done?

Jane sometimes felt these anxieties as well because the process was new to her. Even so, Jane was deeply drawn to the approach and understood that she had an obligation to honor the ways of the individuals she was working with, because the Healing Lodge would house First Nations people. The other regional prisons for women were being planned at the same time in parallel processes, and they were using a more conventional, government-planning approach. As it turns out, the Healing Lodge was the first of all the facilities to open. In the end, the Circle process took less time than the standard process.

This was not an accident. The Circle process creates dialogue that has depth, breadth, and thoroughness. It covers an issue from all sides. It helps a group build the kind of relationships that sustain collective work over long periods of time. And it responds to conflicts in ways that genuinely resolve them, so that bad feelings do not linger. As a result, the decisions coming out of the Circle process are more durable. When the Healing Lodge Planning Circle came to a consensus decision, there was no second-guessing and no resistance to moving forward. No one complained about the decision later on to prove a point. After a consensus decision had been made, the Circle then focused all the group's energies—coherently and single-mindedly—on making the decision work.

The Circle process was used throughout the life of the planning group. All decisions about the Healing Lodge's structure, program, and security were made in Circle. But the Circle was also used for healing—to process emotions and to heal hurts or triggered memories. The teaching Circles continued throughout the process to deepen the understanding of First Nations ways and to strengthen the bonds among participants. The Circle process addressed the physical, mental, emotional, and spiritual needs of the group, especially when challenges arose in any of these areas.

For example, as the only senior federal person representing corrections, Jane felt a heavy burden. The Elders used ceremony to help her unburden herself and realize that she did not need to control the process on behalf of the government. She did not have to bear the burden alone. Indeed, the ceremony served to encourage the rest of the group to bear this responsibility with her and not to see her as the only one responsible for dealing with the government's concerns. The collective wisdom of the group is the strength of the Circle process. Everyone knew that the government's concerns had to be addressed or the project would be blocked. After the ceremony, the entire group committed to finding ways to effectively respond to whatever the government put forward. Jane no longer felt she had to figure this out or make things work on her own.

Shared leadership is a very important part of the Circle process. No individual needs to be all-knowing or all-skillful. No one is single-handedly responsible for the outcome. Every member of the Circle shares in the responsibility for how things go and what the outcome ultimately is.

Not only are Circle decisions more durable, but they are also more creative. Circles access the wisdom of all of the participants. In many ways, the Healing Lodge was the most creative of all five facilities that were built for women serving federal sentences.

The Planning Circle also used celebrations throughout the process. These celebrations honored important steps and re-energized the commitment of the group. For example, after the Elders walked the land that had been chosen, there was a big feast, and several hundred people attended.

For Jane, this was a life-altering experience. It was not easy. Yet the rewards, personally and professionally, have been huge and enduring.

Why Circles Are Such a Good Idea: The Benefits and Potentials of Using Them in Planning

Circles hold enormous potential for use in public planning. Their use brings all sorts of benefits on many levels. We have already described three of the most obvious benefits, which stem from the core of how Circles operate. These three beneficial aspects of the Circle process are:

Circles Are Inclusive

First, everyone can take part in the process. No one is excluded. The Circle starts from the premise that all parties must be included. Everyone's point of view is not only respected but also needed for a good outcome. Circles make us aware of how each person's part fits into the whole. This is a huge benefit, because trouble always arises when people are excluded.

Dominic Barter has been conducting "Restorative Circles" in some of the poorest communities in Brazil. During a seminar held in Saint Paul, Minnesota, he commented that, as long as we strive to be as inclusive as we can, we do not need to worry too much about forgetting someone. "If your expressed intent is to be inclusive and you leave people out," he said, "they will come knocking on your door."

Circles Operate by Consensus

Second, decisions are made by consensus. Although coming to consensus generally takes longer than other forms of decision-making, implementing consensus decisions takes less time, which makes it more efficient in the long run. Such was the case with using Circles to create the Healing Lodge: it opened before any of the other four women's prisons. The Circle process turned out to be more efficient than the conventional process of planning and implementation. Because coming to consensus requires that everyone be treated with respect, that every point of view be heard, and that the relevant needs of every party be met in some way, it has the benefit of building good relations. Also, because the process values dissenting voices, it addresses issues that might not ordinarily be raised early on but that would undoubtedly come up later. The struggle to figure all this out takes time, but it can lead to better decisions. The effort that consensus requires pays off.

Circles Resolve Conflicts

Third, Circles have been used extensively to resolve all sorts of conflicts. One of the Circle's strengths is that it strives to get at the underlying causes of breakdowns in relationships. Circles are highly appropriate even for complex, serious conflicts. When it is most critical to address the underlying causes of a conflict, when major changes in relationships must be made, or when innovative solutions seem hardest to find, the Circle is just the process to use. Circles handle complexity; they spark creativity; and they generate consensus. Not only do they devise changes that no one imagined, they also provide the means for sustaining these changes and seeing that they work over the long haul.

These core dynamics of Circles are by nature beneficial. From them come many other advantages—positive effects that can be particularly valuable in planning. These added benefits describe how Circles shift the dynamics in groups, organizations, and institutions. People respond to each other differently. They see conflicts differently. And the effects of these shifts keep rippling out. For example:

Circles Work from the Bottom Up

By their nature, Circles generate outcomes from the bottom up. All the participants contribute to making a decision or crafting a solution. In virtually every aspect of the process, Circles do not impose things from the top down. Even elements of the process—the values and guidelines—are generated from the bottom up. To deal with a situation, Circles seek to integrate all the concerns. All the factors and all the perspectives go into developing a whole view of the current situation and which course of action seems best.

Circles Balance Individuals and the Collective

Related to this, the Circle holds a balance between the individual and the collective. Circles honor individual needs and gifts, and they simultaneously pay attention to what serves the collective. Integrating what everyone brings to the Circle involves recognizing that each person has gifts and that his or her gifts contribute to the collective.

Circles Deepen Communication

The Circle is a profound tool of communication. The quality of speaking and listening that happens in a Circle is rare in other processes. Seldom do people speak from such a deep place as they are able to do in Circles.

Circles Make the Most of Human Resources

Circles are excellent at maximizing human resources. The Circle brings people together in a way that their assets can complement and support rather than compete with each other. This is essential for good planning. All collective work requires people skills. The Circle hones these for everyone, even those who think they are not good with people. The reason is that the process is rooted in values that characterize good relationships. When everyone in a Circle makes a conscious commitment to these values, they are much more likely to treat each other with respect, honesty, patience, understanding, and compassion. In this environment, people find themselves able to access more of their innate abilities. People skills, technical expertise, openness, and creativity flow in a natural way. No one has to contrive this.

Circles Motivate People

Generating enough motivation is important to the success of any planning effort. The Circle process helps to motivate people in a number of ways. Circles treat everyone's contribution as important. They also strengthen the sense of a shared purpose. Above all, they build relationships that recognize people as whole beings. Supported in these positive ways, a highly motivated group will find solutions to challenges more quickly. People will fulfill their commitments with little oversight, and they will seize opportunities to go above and beyond what is expected of them. All of this builds a momentum that makes the planner's job much easier.

Circles Make the Work Flow More Easily

The Circle supports the everyday work of planning in all sorts of ways. The process brings extremely practical benefits, even administratively. The time invested in Circles can save time many times over. With an ongoing Circle to support a project, tasks can seem to get done almost effortlessly.

For example, by clarifying the common purpose and making it easier for people to share information, Circles prime everyone to engage in the work with more enthusiasm and with a better understanding of what needs to happen. Creativity in solving problems goes up, as does accountability for meeting commitments. Members of the work group feel much more a part of the process, which empowers them.

The shared leadership that the Circle process instills spreads the workload around and reduces the burden on the planning professional. Because group members are clear about the shared purpose and understand how their own tasks contribute to it, the leader is far less likely to feel a need to micromanage others. Trust, confidence, and good feelings build all around.

In a positive atmosphere, work can get done with the greatest ease and efficiency. Not only do people still speak to each other when it is all over, but they also feel a special bond. This comes from having worked through things together in a good way, however hard it may have been.

Circles Handle Problems Constructively

In a Circle, everyone can see how each member is affecting the others and the group as a whole. This is true whether the person's impact on the group seems positive or negative. If the impact is negative, a Circle does not respond with blame or accusations. Rather, Circles focus on problem solving. In such a case, the Circle would respect the dynamics by focusing on what is going on for people, perhaps on a deeper level. What is the issue for the person? What is he or she thinking or feeling? What issues does this experience raise for everyone else? Is the person bringing something to the group's attention that is important but has been unnoticed up to now? How can the negative impact be reversed in an authentic, constructive way?

This form of accountability is generally much more helpful than using the power of structural authority to correct, shame, or punish a person—to make him or her get in line. Such a response is usually adversarial. It creates bad feelings and judgments. Factions form as energies go into arguing about what happened and what people think should have happened. The project itself takes a backseat. All of this has a negative impact on the group as a whole and impedes their ability to work together. Moreover, whatever the real issue might have been in the first place will be more difficult to uncover and handle in a balanced way.

Circles Promote Innovative Thinking

By being inclusive of different views, Circles foster a holistic perspective on things, and this whole-view invites innovative thinking. Each person comes to the Circle carrying his or her own piece of the puzzle. Through the dialogue, participants see how these pieces might fit together and complement each other in unexpected ways. In the article "Mindshift: Strategic Dialogue for Breakthrough Thinking," Juanita Brown and Sherrin Bennett use photography as another metaphor for how this works. Under the heading "Embracing Diverse Perspectives," they write:

> Like a photographer exploring a situation, each comment offers a picture from a different vantage point in an effort to tell the whole story. The whole picture in soft focus brings better understanding than detailed pictures of fragmented parts. Each person adds to the common pool of ideas rather [than] trying to prove or persuade from their own point of

view. Partners in dialogue are challenged to find a *coherent interpretation of their multiple perspectives*. Each comment is seen as true in its own right and as a valuable clue essential to revealing the mystery of the whole. This expectant attitude can ignite the sparks of insight that bring about innovation.[1]

Circles Are Responsive to Changes

Circles are very effective at helping people adapt to unexpected changes. Sometimes the best of plans turn out to be inadequate or completely wrong. When changes need to be made, participants sometimes find it hard to accept them and adjust. A Circle gives them a chance to express their frustrations or the difficulties they see in shifting course. It also helps people identify strategies to make changes easier for them.

Whatever the challenges may be, a Circle eases the tensions that surface around times of change. If change is necessary, a Circle can normalize the adjustment process. Even more, it can help to transform the natural resistance to change into creativity, so that everyone can make the most of the new situation.

Circles Function Organically

The Circle is organic in its approach. It holds a space open for the issues that people bring to the dialogue and does not try to confine the discussion. It does not, for example, try to isolate a particular event from related experiences. The Circle dialogue is open to discussing anything that the participants believe to be relevant in order to address the purpose of the Circle. This approach leads to a holistic look at situations. It also leaves the door open for unexpected insights and for creative possibilities to come out.

Circles Promote Organizational Learning

The Circle provides opportunities for people in organizations to learn from each other. Over time, this develops into group learning, where the members learn together as a team. "Who knows more than whom?" gives way to a shared learning process that motivates everyone. Circles are particularly good at fostering this dynamic, because the process is respectful and reflective—two characteristics that support cooperative learning. The use of the talking piece brings out those who are typically quiet, so that their wisdom contributes to the group. When a group of people share their insights and perspectives on an ongoing basis, they begin to trust each other, and this trust supports learning as well.

Circles Nurture Our Whole Nature

Circles help us bring our whole being to our work. This includes the mental, physical, emotional, and spiritual, meaning-based dimensions of who we are. The more we can integrate all these aspects of our lives, the more competent and effective we will be at what we do, whatever it is. For most people, the values of the Circle process are closely aligned with their sense of meaning and spirituality. By nurturing our value-based "best selves," the Circle brings our work lives into alignment with our spiritual lives, without imposing any specific form of spirituality.

Circles Increase Social Justice

In a larger frame, Circles address core questions about how we organize society: How can we govern ourselves most effectively? How can we make good decisions about how we plan our lives together? By its very nature, the Circle process is a force for social justice, because it is democratic to the core. It gives voice to those whose voices have not been heard. And it treats all parties equally. The Circle does not say to some people, "You lost—too bad, so sad. Get over it. We have the power; you don't. We make the decisions now. Get used to it."

Instead, the Circle says to each member: "Who you are is important. How you see things is important. What you want for your lives and your children is important. What you choose to do as a people is important. This is a place where you can tell your story and be heard. This is a place for us to listen to each other with respect and integrity. Each one of us is an essential part of this process. Each person's concerns are going to be addressed in the outcome. We are all responsible for how this process goes. We will work this process together until we find a resolution that we can all accept and live with." This is a new message for a public process to send.

Circles Invite Transformation

Finally, Circles have a transformative effect. People change; their relationships change; and their communities and organizations change with them. It takes time to integrate a Circle approach into a community. However, with time and use, Circles send out ripples of benefits on all these levels, which together bring transformation. Tapping our potentials for change may well be the greatest, long-term benefit that using Circles can bring.

 CHAPTER TWELVE

Not All Clear Sailing:
Challenges and Cautions

Using Circles clearly offers huge benefits for the public planning pro-cess. However, introducing Circles into a planning department or even a project has its own set of challenges. Since it helps to know what the problems, hurdles, and objections might be, we want to share some words of caution based on our own experiences.

To start, we must keep in mind that the dominant society is un-familiar with the principles and practices of Circles. Therefore, it is natural for people to feel that the Circle process is just too strange or too simple to do much good. The response reflects how we have all been trained. It is not personal. The Circle philosophy about how to "get things done" is quite different from the mainstream approach. We cannot emphasize enough how much of a paradigm shift the Circle process actually is. Circles seem so simple and straightforward, and they are. But they invite us to engage with each other and with issues in ways that are just the opposite of how most of us have been raised, educated, and trained.

The conventional model of management usually relies on chains of command: hierarchical, top-down control. Our educational struc-tures mirror this model to prepare us for working in business, govern-ment, and professional worlds. When we go to work, we ask: Who pays me? Who is my boss? Where is my place in the hierarchy—the organizational flow chart? And what knowledge do I have to master to be able to do my job? If something is not my responsibility, it is not my concern. A holistic view is not valued and nurtured. Indeed, top-down structures suppress a holistic view. Our failure to work from a holistic view results in unacknowledged harm. Worse, the result is that people participate in harmful processes unknowingly, causing harm that they would not choose to do if they were aware.

For decades, thinkers in management science have urged us to move beyond this conventional model. Margaret Wheatley is one such thinker. We would like to share the opening remarks from her article "Leadership Lessons for the Real World":

People often comment that the new leadership I propose couldn't possibly work in "the real world." This "real world" demands efficiency and obedience and is managed by bureaucracy and governed by policies and laws. It is filled with people who do what they're told, who sit passively waiting for instructions, and it relies on standard operating procedures for every situation, even when chaos erupts and things are out of control.

This real world was invented by Western thought. We believe that people, organizations, and the world are machines, and we can organize massive systems to run like clockwork in a steady-state world. The leader's job is to create stability and control, because without human intervention, there is no hope for order. It is assumed that most people are dull, not creative, that people need to be bossed around, that new skills only develop through training. People are motivated using fear and rewards; internal motivators such as compassion and generosity are discounted.

This is not the real world. The *real* real world demands that we learn to cope with chaos, that we understand what motivates humans, that we adopt strategies and behaviors that lead to order, not more chaos.

Here is the real world described by new science. It is a world of interconnected networks, where slight disturbances in one part of the system create major impacts far from where they originate. In this highly sensitive system, the most minute actions can blow up into massive disruptions and chaos. But it is also a world that seeks order. When chaos erupts, it not only destroys the current structure, it also creates the conditions for new order to emerge. Change always involves a dark night when everything falls apart. Yet if this period of dissolution is used to create new meaning, then chaos ends and new order emerges.

This is a world that knows how to organize itself without

command and control or charisma. Everywhere, life self-organizes as networks of relationships. When individuals discover a common interest or passion, they organize themselves and figure out how to make things happen. Self-organizing evokes creativity and leads to results, creating strong, adaptive systems. Surprising new strengths and capacities emerge.

In this world, the "basic building blocks" of life are relationships, not individuals. Nothing exists on its own or has a final, fixed identity. We are all "bundles of potential" (as one scientist described quantum particles). Relationships evoke these potentials. We change as we meet different people or are in different circumstances.

In this historic moment, we live caught between the mechanical worldview that no longer works and a new paradigm that we fear to embrace. But this new paradigm comes with the promise that it can provide solutions to our most unsolvable challenges.[1]

Except for emergencies—and even then it is debatable—the top-down approach is losing credibility with many people as the wisest or most effective way to get things done. For one thing, it severely narrows the pool of knowledge and experience on which decisions are made. For another, it makes enormous systems—systems that affect the lives of millions or even billions of people—extremely vulnerable to the decisions of a few at the top. Keeping the holistic view the exclusive domain of a few has allowed for massive abuses. It has also led to bad judgments with catastrophic results.

Yet in spite of management consultants arguing long and hard for the benefits of "servant leadership," "team learning," "shared visions," and "whole-system thinking," it is still easy to slip into the assumption that top-down decision-making is the best way to go. It can seem like the "most efficient" way—the way to "get things done."

Given this cultural context, it is no wonder that many aspects of Circles seem odd to people when they first experience the process. "Who moved all the chairs around?" "Where are all the tables?" "Why do we have to hold something to be able to speak?" "Why are we spending all this time talking about values?" "Is hearing this story about this person's ancestors really necessary for us to decide where to build the new mall?"

Beyond these immediate reactions, what can seem most strange to newcomers is the space that Circles create for genuinely egalitarian, democratic dialogue. Many people have never experienced being in such a space before. It takes time to adjust. We are accustomed either to being told what to do or to telling others what to do. Someone is always in control. Spending time in a place of uncertainty and indecision? Listening to all sides? Not knowing what the outcome might be until everyone in the group agrees to a course? This takes some getting used to. Participants in Circles have to adapt to a different way of being together, and they have to trust that the process is worth doing.

If we want to introduce Circles into a planning process, we need to consider where people are coming from. What have their experiences been around getting things done before, whether at work or in communities? What are they assuming and expecting as a result? How might we present the Circle process in a good way, so that it has the greatest likelihood of being accepted? In other words, how might we bridge people's lack of experience with Circles—and decades of conditioning in another paradigm—so that they can begin to appreciate what Circles offer and be willing to participate in them?

Being Flexible about Terminology

When we experience something new, we feel uncomfortable at first. Objecting to terms or word usage is an easy way to express our discomfort. In promoting Circles, we can be sensitive to people's reactions to Circle terminology. Perhaps the terms are triggering something distressing from past experiences, or maybe people are feeling cynical about something that looks like the latest mediation technique. Their reactions may also reflect the discomfort that comes with undergoing a paradigm shift.

Whatever the reason, the language that reflects the Circle's Indigenous origins need not be a stumbling block for newcomers to the process. We can use other terms. If terms such as "Circle," "ceremony," or "talking piece" pose an obstacle, we can describe what we are doing differently. The success of the Circle process does not depend on the words we use. What matters is the intention to practice the Circle's underlying principles: valuing each voice, sharing leadership, holding each other mutually accountable, making decisions by consensus, and returning to commonly held values. Terminology need not be a barrier to practicing these underlying principles. If it helps in some professional or organizational contexts to adapt the terms we use to make these principles more accessible, then we should do this.

We might also want to introduce the process one step at a time. We might arrange for people to sit in a circle as a first step without using other parts of the process. There is power in the geometry. It moves people away from the old paradigm. Using a talking piece has a similar effect. These two elements have an inherent power to spur shifts away from the conventional model of interacting. These elements do not take us all the way to the potential of Circles, but they are powerful enough to point people in new directions. When we make these changes, we do not have to use the term "Circle" or "talking piece." Even without engaging the full Circle process, such simple changes in a meeting can contribute to fundamental shifts in how people communicate. The group dynamics will change.

The Road to Public and Political Acceptance

Our societies have public and political processes that are familiar to us. Although we may criticize them, they provide a certain baseline of expectations. We know what to expect, for example, when we attend a council session or a public meeting. We know our roles, whether we come as a politician, a staff person, or a member of the public. We know who has authority over what; we know whether or not we can speak; and if we are allowed to speak, we know when we can do so.

By contrast, the Circle process is new for most non-Indigenous people. It requires explanation, time, and experience before it begins to feel natural. At first, the actual experience may seem disquieting, if not downright uncomfortable. For those in positions of power, for example, the equality of the Circle may feel threatening. Politicians may not like changing their role from speakers to listeners and from authority figures to equal participants. Conversely, members of the public may not be used to speaking in front of authority figures and being taken seriously.

For these reasons, it is important for organizers to explain the Circle process thoroughly before asking people to participate in it. Even then, we should be prepared for some initial discomfort or outright resistance. Using Circles in planning will require various stages of education about the process. We need to build a general awareness about how Circles work, what they can do, and why they are so effective.

We believe that perceptions about Circles will change, because we have seen it happen. Granted, it takes more time for some folks than for others, since just about everything is different about the process. For example, what do we mean when we say that a process is "effective"? Do we mean that it enables us to push through a plan as quickly as possible? Or is a process "effective" when it enables us to develop a plan that incorporates many viewpoints and thereby creates a broad base of community support? As more people experience the Circle process, a momentum for using Circles will build. Over time, we envision that Circles will become more widely understood and accepted.

Confronting the Risks

As many of us have learned, introducing a new idea involves a certain amount of risk, personally and professionally. One's personality, position, and authority in an organization influence how much risk we may be willing or able to take. Some circumstances for using Circles are less risky than others.

For example, the young planner who was excited about using the Circle with unemployed youth was much more hesitant to use it with the local city council. She made a comment that probably hits home for many planners: "I have worked so hard to get credibility as a planner. I feel I would be 'laughed off the stage' if I suggested a Circle." Planners have to assess these risks case by case.

Even when a situation seems too risky for a newer planner, more established planners might be receptive because the risk for them is less. Their standing gives them a measure of authority and protection. In fact, they might enjoy the challenge of learning a new process and introducing something innovative.

Some planners might wonder whether using Circles to engage the public might increase the risk of "bad" outcomes. For example, we all realize that urban sprawl is the result of poorly planned communities. Nonetheless, many people prefer urban sprawl because it is what they know. If we bring in many people who are not planning professionals and who have been raised in unwise, unsustainable land-use patterns, will we end up with more of the same? Will we be able to plan wisely and make the changes that energy consumption and the environment, for example, are urging us to make? These are important questions to consider.

Sometimes the decisions may not be the best. However, because Circles bring together diverse people and perspectives—including planners and other professionals—the use of Circles makes it more likely that all views will be heard. Plus, if a change is advisable from a professional perspective that upsets the community's existing habits, Circles can provide a forum for public education and dialogue about the value of the proposed change. Circles can help generate the community support that a new design needs. And they can help planners think through considerations—legitimate concerns—that even the most thorough planners might miss. Unlike other public processes, Circles operate on an equality of voice. This prevents one person—pro or con—from dominating or grandstanding to force through an agenda.

The Unexpected: Coping with One's Lack of Experience

As we explained in chapters 5 and 7, some types of Circles can be conducted quite successfully without formal training. If you decide to start this way—i.e., to organize a Circle before you have had a chance to attend a Circle training—we suggest that you begin with Circles that are relatively easy. Avoid topics that have an obvious potential for conflict. Holding Circles among friends and colleagues or within your office—some "safe" group—is also an easy way to begin.

However, even the most seemingly predictable or innocuous Circle can bring surprises. Because Circles create a safe space where people speak from the heart, there is always the potential for unexpected information or intense emotions to come out. First of all, this is a sign not that a Circle is not working but that it is. The Circle is providing a space for participants to deal with issues that are pressing in their lives. Most likely, they do not have other places where they can deal with these issues or express these emotions with the depth that Circles make possible.

Yet what do you do in such a case? For keepers who have not received Circle training—and even for those who are trained but have limited experiences—the situation may well feel scary. It might also cause you to second-guess yourself or to question whether it was a good idea to hold the Circle at all. Having been there ourselves, we would suggest that you keep the following points in mind.

- The Circle does not create the emotions that arise; it allows people to become aware of feelings they may not have known before and to learn from them through the witnessing of others.
- Any public process comes with the risk that strong emotions might be expressed.

With these considerations in mind, what can you do?

- Take people back to the values and guidelines established at the beginning.
- Turn the situation or issue back to the Circle group for guidance on how to proceed. Don't default into thinking that you need to control the process. You also don't need to try to resolve the issue or find a solution. Being present and holding a safe space for whatever process needs to go on is all that you are here to do. And you do not do this alone. Everyone in the Circle shares responsibility for how Circles unfold.
- Make sure that there is enough time for the Circle to adequately respond to whatever has come up. Be prepared to stay longer or arrange to meet again on another day, so the discussion is not left hanging.
- If the discussion has triggered issues of prior victimization (i.e., experiences of prejudice, discrimination, or violence) for any participants, be prepared to refer them to a counselling resource or to some other form of help and support. Putting the issue back on the Circle also draws on the group's knowledge and experience of outside resources.

- Contact someone who is more experienced in the Circle process to give you feedback, insight, and support.
- If you decide to use Circles more often and in increasingly diverse settings, you might want to attend a Circle training and do further reading (see appendices 2 and 3).

And then, it is also true that Circles are not for every occasion. If you have chosen to use a Circle and then sense that it was not the best choice, you can always say so and put the decision to the group. Randy French recalls such an experience:

> One time, I was involved in facilitating a meeting on a controversial development, and I was using the Circle. But it did not feel right, so I just had to stop and apologize. I took responsibility for trying to use the Circle process and suggested that, though the issue was important, it was not appropriate for being resolved by using the Circle.

Again, Circles are more than a technique. They embody a philosophy, a mindset, and a way of life. The more the way of Circles becomes a part of who we are, the easier it is for us to trust the process and respond intuitively in a Circle-based way.

Planners as Circle Facilitators and Participants: New Roles

Another difference about Circles that planners might find risky is that, as keepers, we have to give up some of our control. In more conventional styles of facilitating a group process, the facilitator plays a major role in what happens and hence also in determining the outcome. By contrast, the Circle keeper's role is simply to guide and offer direction; the real control is shared among the participants.

As professional planners, we have definite expectations put on us. This is part of our job. It is not at all unreasonable, then, for planners to consider very carefully the wisdom of giving up some of our control. Is this a smart move? How will it affect the overall outcome? There is no escaping these questions if we want to use Circles.

Straddling the fence does not work. We cannot both use Circles and retain the same level of control. The more we try to control a

Circle, the more it will become like any other facilitated process. The more we relinquish control and trust the Circle, the more we will experience the full potential that Circles offer.

This takes practice, though, because it means we have to set aside, at least for a time, much of our personal and professional programming. So many of us were not only raised but also professionally trained to be in control as much as possible. We feel as if we are incompetent or failing in our responsibilities if we do not have all the answers. Presumably, our job is to fix things and provide solutions. To let this go and invite others into the process is new.

In Circles, planners are equal participants, whether we function as a keeper or as a Circle member. Like everyone else, we are expected to bring our ideas, concerns, knowledge, and expertise to the dialogue. We are invited to speak from our hearts and not just from our "objective," rational minds. For many professionals—and certainly for planners—this is unfamiliar territory. We are trained to maintain a professional distance and to operate intellectually. Above all, planners are expected to stay removed from the passions and emotions that fuel many planning issues. No question, Circles present challenges for planners. Yet they also give us a chance to learn a new mode of practice. And they give us a way to engage the public that is genuinely respectful and collaborative.

One of the roles of a keeper is to model the kind of dialogue that Circles invite. Circles encourage participants, for example, to speak from their personal experiences and to avoid lecturing the group. One of the most important roles that keepers have is modeling this kind of communication—speaking from their hearts and keeping their remarks rooted in their own experiences.

If planners—especially those who serve as keepers—are uncomfortable with this role, they fall back on speaking from a detached professionalism. In doing so, though, it may seem as if they are trying to control the process. Moreover, the conversation is less likely to go beyond an intellectual level. The experience will resemble other conventionally facilitated processes.

By contrast, when keepers model a more experiential, heart-centered expression, they give others permission to follow suit. People start taking risks by talking about what is most meaningful to them. They share what they feel strongly about and tell the personal stories that led them to these views.

Finally, the role of keepers includes a commitment to caring for the well-being of all the participants. This may mean following up with some of the members after a Circle, particularly if you observed that the process was difficult for them. You may want to check in to make sure that they are okay afterward. Engaging with community members at this level may be new and unfamiliar to some planners, but it contributes to building the safe space that Circles can hold.

Time and Efficiency: Dealing with the Constraints

Of course, given the values of our society, we all feel a certain pressure to get things done in a timely and efficient manner. Reports need to be written and plans designed and approved. Time management and efficiency are important. However, they are often valued above the relationships that hold communities and societies together. These are the very relationships that make any decision work in the long run. What is saved in time and efficiency may well be lost because solid relationships have not been formed between the planners and those most affected by the plans.

Circles do not have to take excessive amounts of time; they can be limited to the time available. But even when the process is lengthy and time-consuming, in a larger sense, Circles ultimately save time. Long-time Circle keepers can give all sorts of examples that prove this point. The outcomes are more balanced, because they weave in more perspectives. As a result, the decisions that come out of a Circle process usually have more "buy-in." This is true even for members who did not totally agree with the outcome. The very fact that their views were listened to and considered in a substantive way makes a difference. And if their views did not find their way into the outcome, they understand why.

Randy French describes how he used the Circle process within the time restraints of a conference setting to maximize the input from participants:

> At a recent "Lake Planning" conference for Lake Superior, I wanted to hear from everyone on four main questions, so I divided a group of twenty-four into breakout groups of six each, one for each question. Each group formed their own Circle, so everyone could voice their opinion on answering

the questions. In the end, everyone had their say on all four questions and was able to offer their input. I walked away with sixty pages of ideas and suggestions on developing a lake plan for Lake Superior. This document isn't static either, like the minutes of a meeting. It is fluid and can be added to and expanded on as people reflect on other ideas. I love the process, because it gets people to take ownership and buy into an idea.

Documenting the Results

The kind of public processes in which planners are involved often need to be documented. We need to produce minutes, for example, that explain what happened and what, if anything, was decided. One challenge with using Circles is figuring out the best way to provide a written report. How can we incorporate the group's input into a written document? Actually, we have a number of options. Many Circles used in other contexts must develop formal agreements. For example, Circles are often used to address harms that have occurred between victims and offenders. In these contexts, the court requires that a Circle make certain agreements (i.e., social compacts or an actual sentence) about how to address the harm and mend it. Planners can incorporate some of the more formal aspects of this work into the less formal, more conversational structure of most planning Circles.

Specifically, it is important to let everyone know up front how the meeting is going to be recorded. Using flip charts, for example, is one way to record comments as the Circle progresses. Participants can then see how their comments are being recorded and can come to a consensus about the final form. Another way is to give someone the job of taking notes. At the end, these notes may be read back into the Circle. The group can then agree about what to make public and how to say it. If a Circle is part of a formal public process, the keeper will need to explain the need to keep a public record of who attended and the comments that were made.

Confidentiality raises special concerns. It is a shared value in many Circles, and it raises challenges when it comes to recording what was said. When confidentiality is an issue, participants will need to discuss what goes into the report and what stays out. How can personal information be protected while making a public record? Each Circle must decide.

How Many People Can Participate?

Can there be either too many or too few people in a Circle? Couples now use Circles or its principles to enhance their communication, so two people are not too few. The best or optimal size of a Circle depends on the Circle's purpose. When organizers personally invite the participants, the group's size is predictable. The goal is to include those who have a concern or interest in the issue and its outcome or who might serve as a resource. Most Circles include somewhere between five and twenty people.

In public forums, however, organizers cannot be sure how many people will attend until the time arrives. In such cases, we have to be prepared to change our procedures, so that everyone has a chance to participate. If enough people who can serve as keepers are present, more than one Circle might be used to accommodate everyone. Circles have been used with as many as two hundred people, though this size obviously limits the input that each person can make.

When large numbers of people show up, keepers can incorporate elements of the Circle even if they cannot pass the talking piece to everyone. For example, we can engage the group in an opening ceremony and invite a discussion of values and guidelines. We can put out questions for everyone to consider, and then we can try to make sure that all sides of an issue are represented in a respectful way. For example, we can invite people to speak whose perspectives have not been expressed so far. With particularly large numbers of participants, not everyone will get a chance to speak, so we must be especially attentive to making sure that a diversity and balance of perspectives are expressed. Whatever happens, we can be sure to close the meeting with a positive sense of what went on. Planners will have to use their creativity here in acknowledging what has been accomplished.

Will Circles Raise False Hopes?

For planners, Circles offer a new and different approach to their work. They give us a way to collaborate with other professionals, politicians, and the general public in shaping our future. Through Circles, we receive input from people on issues that matter to them. We hear them in a way that we might otherwise lack the means to do. Circles create a space in which confrontations and adversarial dynamics give way to joined efforts. As people listen to each other's concerns, they shift their focus to the deeper issues. Then they begin to rally their creativity to find solutions that can work for everyone.

This process holds great promise. Yet in our personal experiences, the more we incorporated Circle principles into our planning practices, the more we began to worry. Will we raise people's hopes too high? Will the public develop unrealistic expectations about what the process can offer? People have a chance to provide all this great input. What if nothing changes?

One way to address these concerns is to keep Circle participants focused on the job at hand. At the beginning of each Circle, keepers can define the Circle's particular purpose. We can spell out what we are hoping to achieve and what role the Circle will play in the overall decision-making process. Planning processes occur within larger systems that cannot always be controlled or changed. Part of our job is to help people understand up front what is within our power to change through Circles and what may not be within our power. This lessens the risk of the community feeling betrayed after they engaged with the process in such an authentic way.

Although in a planning context Circles may not make the final decision, they can still influence the decision. For example, if everyone agrees to it in advance, the outcome of any Circle process may be used as input for the next stages of planning. Another option is to invite decision-makers to a Circle, so that they can hear all the information as well as the range of perspectives on an issue. This gives decision-makers, particularly elected officials, a chance to experience Circles firsthand and to become committed to the process. Sitting in a Circle and listening to multiple perspectives may then inform the decisions they make in the future.

These are some of the more specific challenges that we have experienced in introducing Circles into public planning, as well as some suggestions about how to meet these challenges. In general, the best response is to go back to Circle principles and values—to its philosophy—and then to explore how this framework might serve as a guide.

Obviously, being exclusive, disrespectful, partial, or controlling is not going to create a Circle-based response. On the other hand, it is not always clear how we can be most inclusive, respectful, egalitarian, or open to shared leadership. Our lifetime of experiences in a more controlling paradigm will kick in, often when we least expect it. We will make mistakes and wish we had handled things differently.

Yet in the bigger picture, all this is natural. It is just part of learning a new process and making a paradigm shift. The only real danger would be to allow these experiences to make us give up on using Circles. As long as we keep going back to Circle basics and integrating them with our work in whatever ways we can, these challenges tend to sort themselves out.

Can We Risk Doing Democracy?

At this point, we would like to step back and consider one last challenge to using Circles—a philosophical challenge. Circles represent a paradigm shift toward practicing democracy to a profound degree. Can we actually be as democratic as Circles are? We come back to the issues around democracy that we raised in the introduction.

If we look for examples of democracies in history, we can find full participatory ones that have been successful and enduring. As Chief Oren Lyons explained, the Haudenosaunee League of Six Nations in northeastern North America has practiced a profound democracy for untold generations. Even children vote on decisions, since every decision affects their futures. Indeed, it was the Haudenosaunee model that inspired Benjamin Franklin and other U.S. founders to push for a more democratic form of government than existed in most of Europe at the time. The United States Constitution with its three branches of government held in balance borrows heavily from the Haudenosaunee model.

In Europe, Switzerland is often pointed to as a model of full participatory democracy and has been using this model since 1291 CE. Town hall meetings in New England offer another form of direct democracy. In direct democracies, citizens participate in decision-making directly. In representative democracies, people are elected or appointed to represent citizens in the decision-making.

Circles provide a tool that can significantly deepen and expand the practice of direct democracy. But can we trust direct democracies to arrive at good decisions? This is a very old question that political philosophers East and West have wrestled with. Once again, we come up against the question: Can direct democracies really work?

The Issue of Human Nature

In the West, concerns about the viability of direct democracies have stemmed from different views of human nature. Those who have seen human nature as being heavily controlled by greed and self-interest have understandably doubted that a just, fair, and equitable society would come from direct citizen participation.

Seventeenth-century British political philosopher Thomas Hobbes, for example, is known for describing human beings as a selfish, greedy, power-driven species. His solution was to install a monarchy that possessed nearly absolute, top-down authority and control. Since Hobbes knew full well that such absolute power would inevitably lead to abuses, he hoped that the monarchy could be held in check by a limited form of representative democracy.[2]

China's classic Legalist philosopher, Han Fei Tzu, argued similarly nearly two thousand years before Hobbes.[3] He argued for an all-powerful state to contain the side of human beings that makes us prone to exploit and hurt each other. The state does this by instituting laws that apply to everyone. Certainly the decisions and patterns of behavior that led to the financial meltdown in 2008 and 2009 suggest that these concerns about human nature are not outdated.

This, then, is the philosophical challenge: If our nature is prone to pursue self-interest at cost to others, can general citizens be trusted to make good, balanced, equitable, and informed decisions? In other words, can the level of democracy that Circles practice really work?

The Consequences of Exclusion

The Western response to this issue has been to privilege one group of people with economic, social, educational, political, and professional advantages. This privileged group could then be entrusted with the decisions that affect the rest of society. This is why most European-dominant modern states have representative democracies instead of direct ones. As we mentioned in the introduction, in the founding of the United States, only landed white men were allowed to vote. All people of color, all women, all children, all poor white men, and certainly all non-human species were excluded from the decision-making processes.

Yet excluding entire peoples from the decision-making has led to massive harms. Our histories demonstrate how profound these issues are and what can be at stake when those involved with planning use a decision-making process that is not inclusive. As planners are keenly aware, the function of planning is an essential part of society, and it powerfully shapes what happens "on the ground."

When those most affected by a planning policy or decision are not given a voice in the decision-making process, the results can cause considerable harm to the community. Planning in the broadest social sense has, in some contexts, created injustices that have caused suffering and harm for generations to follow. It might help to step back and consider these, even though planning as a profession did not exist when many of these harms occurred. These historical examples show what can happen when societies make major, long-range planning decisions without including those whose lives will be most affected or first gaining their consent. For example:

- In the United States, no Cherokee, Dakota, Diné, Apache, Choctaw, Cheyenne, or any other Native People would ever have agreed to their "forced removal" from their homelands. The invading and occupying "settler society" made this "land use" and "planning" decision unilaterally.
- In both the United States and Canada, Native Peoples and First Nations would not have chosen residential boarding schools to raise their children—another long-term planning policy designed to eradicate Indigenous cultures and to establish the dominance of Eurocentric societies.
- Neither would Native Peoples—or indeed the buffalo themselves—have agreed to the extermination of forty to sixty million buffalo so that cattle ranching and wheat

production could dominate the Central Plains. This "land-use policy" promoted the extermination of Native Peoples as well, given their dependence on bison.

- African Americans would not have agreed to plantation slavery, industrial slavery, Jim Crow laws, or substandard housing and education—segregation being another core planning issue for a society.

- Black South Africans would not have chosen apartheid as the best form of rule in the land of their ancestors—again, land use and planning being a central social issue.

- People of low income most likely would not choose to see their neighborhoods gentrified. The higher property values, rents, and taxes associated with more affluent people moving into a neighborhood tend to force those of lesser economic means to leave.

All these voices had to be excluded from the decision-making to allow these planning policies to be made and then carried out. Because the decisions excluded the voices of those most affected—and affected extremely negatively—the policies often had to be implemented through the use of force.

We cite these examples to underscore the power of the planning function in the largest societal context. These examples also show how momentous and devastating the choice to include or exclude people from the decision-making process can be.

Obviously, many of these injustices occurred before the planning profession was founded in the early twentieth century. However, for many economically disadvantaged communities or communities of color, patterns of exclusion from decision-making continue today. The result is that injustices continue as well. Ethan Goffman describes the ongoing situation in the article "Industry and Environmental Justice: Can a Historic Black Neighborhood Be Preserved?":

This industrial encroachment dating back decades is proto-typical for African American neighborhoods, says Robert Bullard, director of the Environmental Justice Center at Clark Atlanta University. Bullard, known as the father of the environmental justice movement, paints a picture of how politically influential, largely white neighborhoods have long resisted undesirable development, which ends up in neighborhoods without a voice in local government.

"Whether it's highways or freeways, bus barns, diesel buses or fighting to get access to metro stops, African American areas have been short-changed," says Bullard. "Tax and transportation dollars end up disenfranchising black communities."

Lincoln Park resident and civic association member Wilma Bell echoes Bullard's sentiment. In black neighborhoods, industrial encroachment is "historically what happens," she says. "We always have to fight."[4]

The struggles of Indigenous Peoples to preserve their homelands continue all over the world. In the United States, much of the land retained by Native Peoples was deemed worthless to whites at the time the treaties were made. These same lands are now found to be rich with oil, coal, uranium, minerals, and other sources of wealth in a capitalist commodity system. The "land use and planning" battles go on.

The Parameters of the Planners' Role

Though the scope of public planning is immense and its consequences can be devastating, the role that we as planners have in the larger process is limited. The broad function of planning in a society decides who can do or build what—when, where, and how. As a result, planning policies determine who lives where, how resources will be used, and who has access to land and resources. Though elected officials are generally responsible for decision-making and establishing broad policies, we as planners are nonetheless part of the process. Our job is to implement planning policies—both those that we often develop and those that are adopted by officials in government.

Part of our work in implementing policies is to solicit public input. We then participate in weighing this input relative to the policies that are to be implemented. Collecting feedback from communities is a fundamental part of what we do. If, in the process of implementing public planning policy, we discover clear public opposition, our job as planners is to work with these concerns, seek solutions and information, and strive to educate the decision makers.

At some point in our careers, most of us have found ourselves in the difficult position of having to implement policies that we disagreed with and that at times called us into an advocacy role. Yet even in such difficult situations, though our job instructs us to follow the direction set by public policy-makers, we can nonetheless influence how policies are written, and we can make recommendations.

From a systems perspective, being part of a system gives us power to change it, hence also a choice about how to use this power. One choice we often have is choosing the process for public consultation. This choice, in turn, reflects a deeper choice about how inclusive our decision-making process can afford to be.

In systems that involve change, growth, and learning, feedback plays a critical role. In planning, feedback is essential to developing a good plan—one that works for everyone involved. So, as planners, we regularly face the question: How inclusive shall we be in seeking feedback on any given plan or policy? We can only imagine that, had we as societies been able to hear the feedback from those most affected by the unjust "planning" policies of the past, we as societies could have avoided committing such severe and long-standing injustices.

A Paradigm Shift to Inclusion

Without doubt, human nature is complicated. We have all witnessed our capacities to hurt each other. We have reason to be afraid of what humans can do. And it makes sense that we need some kind of positive framework in order to enjoy peaceful coexistence.

But historical examples of injustices such as those we cited suggest that excluding people from the decision-making is not a solution. It does not produce respectful coexistence. Powerful dictators or absolute state control do not lessen our capacities to hurt each other. Groups of privileged people do not make decisions in the best interests of everyone. Even if these groups were benevolent in intent, how can they know what is best for others?

We raise these issues because of the school of thought that advises us to be suspicious of the public and to keep them out of the decision-making process as much as possible. It almost goes against a certain strain of our conditioning to invite people—the community, regular folks—into the planning process. Shouldn't these decisions be left to experts and authorities? If too many people get involved, aren't we asking for trouble? A part of us might really wonder whether Circles are, in fact, such a good idea.

When these concerns come up, our response has been that, yes, Circles pose a true paradigm shift. This shift changes both how we understand human nature and how we respond to conflicts. The premise of a Circle approach is that our nature is neither all good nor all bad. We span a spectrum of potentials. We obviously can act badly and hurt each other, but we can also be much more. This is true for all of us, both those in power and those in the public, those privileged and those oppressed. Circles are about creating spaces where the better nature that we all have can be expressed and find support. To benefit most from our differences and our potentials, we need public processes that are inclusive and that call forth the best in us. Circles are designed to do both.

Valuing Conflicts and Making the Most of Them

As for conflicts, a Circle philosophy views them as a part of life. Conflicts tell us that life is more complex than we realized. They give us a chance to see differences in a way that we did not see before. We can use conflicts to rearrange our lives on a broader foundation. The interesting questions to ask, then, are

- What differences are coming to light that we have not yet seen or grasped?
- How can we learn from differences and create a better coexistence as a result?
- How can we turn conflicts around, so that they serve our mutual advantage?
- How can we support each other in expressing more of who we are—in being more than selfish, fearful, and all the rest?

Again, Circles are designed to help us explore these questions—questions that planners face all the time—in open, positive, and creative ways.

When we respond to conflicts from the end of our spectrum of potentials that puts us in a fighting mode, it is harder to respond to these questions in creative or constructive ways. A polarized stance takes over. It becomes more difficult for both sides to learn from the other. It is also more difficult to turn the conflict around, so that it serves some mutual good. The adversarial response tends to escalate, shifting the fight to larger scales.

No matter who wins, the outcome is one-sided. The knowledge and experiences of those who lose are excluded from the outcome. What they brought to the conflict is not used to construct a better result. Because the conflict has not been addressed in a holistic way—a way that speaks to all the complexities that gave rise to it—the energies behind the conflict will most likely resurface.

Creating Spaces to Access More of Who We Are

It is natural for conflicts to trigger a fight response. And sometimes fighting is all we can do. When powerful interests set their sites on a community for its resources or as a place to get rid of waste, fighting through grassroots organizing is the primary means of defense. The call to fight warrants respect. Most likely, some rights and concerns have not been adequately acknowledged. Some harm or injustice may well be afoot. Fighting brings issues to our attention, yet it can take us only so far. Somewhere along the line, those in conflict need to listen to each other to come up with a different response.

Fortunately, there is a whole spectrum of human nature from which to craft a response to conflicts. Which other parts of human nature people can call on at these times has to do with how they are "held." If people feel secure and respected, it is easier for them to explore options beyond fighting. We can exercise a wider range of our abilities.

The Circle process forms a safe context that enables participants to do precisely that, namely, to access more of who we are. Circles build a net of relationships that helps us connect with our whole selves, no matter where our emotions may be along the spectrum. They also give us opportunities to speak and act from our best values, especially when conflicts arise.

Listening to others, we begin to see how much we have in common and how we are related. Our natures as human beings are not all that different, however different we may be in other ways. We all love those close to us, for example, and we all want our children to have a good future. We all want our planet to be healthy. This commonality as human beings can give us an incentive to work together.

It is not, then, the way of Circles to tell us to stop fighting. Rather, Circles create a space where the reasons motivating the fight can be acknowledged. Once that is accomplished—not superficially but in a deep and holistic way—the desire to fight shifts to a desire to work together toward a resolution. The energies move naturally. The process is organic, not manipulated or imposed. We start calling on other capacities that we have but which the urge to fight did not allow to surface.

Transforming Conflicts from the Inside Out

Circles address the problem that Han Fei Tzu, Hobbes, and other political philosophers have raised, therefore, not by imposing order and control from without, but by shifting the dynamics from within. Discussing values and agreeing on guidelines are successful for this reason: they work from the inside out. So, too, do many other aspects of the Circle process. Circles strengthen our connection to our inner moral compass. Then they bring our moral compasses together to chart a good course.

Some Indigenous teachings observe that our abilities to access our strengths—our full nature—are reinforced if we can access them together. Consider the metaphor that one arrow can be broken easily, but many arrows bound together can endure greater stress. In the United States, for example, this Indigenous image was incorporated into the "Great Seal," which is on the back of every U.S. one-dollar bill. Similarly, one person's knowledge or moral compass might be off. But when many people's moral compasses point in a direction, chances are the decision is a good one. The decision is likely to be stronger, more balanced, and more sustainable than a decision made by one person alone.

If we take this reasoning a step further, a decision made by a diverse group of people will probably embody more wisdom than a decision made by a group of people who see things roughly the same way. To a Circle mind-set, differences are an asset, which is why conflicts are so valuable. Circles give us the means to learn from our differences to the fullest. We can use them to create a better coexistence and, in the process, to express more of who we are.

⁓

If who we are at our worst is the reason for not including the public in the decision-making process, then Circles can address this issue. Circles embody millennia of wisdom about how to help us bring our whole selves to the dialogue. They hold people in a good way even as we work through complex and emotionally charged issues.

In planning, this means that Circles give us a way to do democracy to a degree yet unknown. This is a good thing, because the more inclusive we can be in our planning processes, the better our chances of making choices that are fair and just for all concerned. John W. Gardner, the founder of Common Cause, said, "The play of conflicting interests in a framework of shared purposes is the drama of a free society." Rooted in this idea, Circles give us a means to open the doors to "citizen participation"—the call that Sherry Arnstein made to planners decades ago.

CHAPTER THIRTEEN

Strengthening Communities: How Circles Promote Community Health

Communities and planning go together. Communities need good planning, and good planning builds healthy and just communities. Circles are a natural fit, because they are a community-based process—profoundly so. As a result, Circles can play a critical role in helping planners strengthen the communities we serve.

Circles do this in a number of ways. In general, Circles build the skills that communities need to manage and regulate their own affairs. The process empowers communities, so that they can determine their own course. As people take back their power from experts or government leadership, they feel greater ownership about what happens in their lives.

Building Community Skills

This community-building starts with individuals. Circles help us develop the personal skills we need to build communities. For example, Circles improve our listening skills. We must be able to listen to each other—really, deeply listen—to create a healthy, functioning community. Circles also deepen our awareness of each other's needs and help us learn how to take care of each other in healthy, respectful ways. We learn how to help each other without losing ourselves in the helping—without either sacrificing our own well-being or further disempowering those needing help. In Circles, we take responsibility for communicating our own needs and for offering our gifts to the group—and everyone has both needs and gifts to offer.

By helping us build relationships across differences, Circles create what is called "social capital." In other words, a strong community makes resources available to individuals and families when they

Housing projects in a community involve complex planning decisions. Wilder Square, Inc., in Saint Paul, Minnesota, is a 163-unit multicultural, cooperative family housing community for low to moderate income adults and families. Low and moderate income housing projects often face opposition, and planners must find constructive ways to work this out.

need help with their day-to-day struggles. The community serves as a bank where people can go to give and receive support. People are prepared to be there for each other. Here again, Circles help us learn how to find a balance between meeting the needs of other community members and meeting our own needs.

By helping members become more aware of each other's needs and interests, Circles make it easier for us to find common ground. This is essential when conflicts arise, as they do in any community. Circles help us see the good things that can come out of conflicts, which inspires us to respond to them with more openness and in more balanced ways. This also reduces the tendency to suppress or flee from conflicts. Not only does such a response often make things worse, but it also deprives us of the good that the conflict could hold for everyone involved.

These are some of the ways that Circles prepare us as individuals to step into our roles as community members. In a planning context, community members with Circle experience can be a great asset. When a planner is arranging a Circle, these community members can be called on to participate, even if the issue does not relate to them personally. By modeling their knowledge of Circles, they can help those new to the process adjust to a Circle approach.

In fact, community members—"third parties"—can play extremely valuable roles in Circles.[1] They balance the dialogue, so that those in direct conflict are not the only ones speaking. They can also serve as keepers, thus demonstrating community empowerment. The community is not dependent on having outside professionals come in and run the Circles.

The role of community members has been an important factor in the Bluewater case concerning water quality (presented in chapter 8). The parties in conflict were able to trust the process, in part, because community members could serve as the keepers and organizers of the Circles. In addition, these community members served as advocates for the process. They were comfortable enough with the process to encourage others to learn it and to participate in Circles. The experience showed everyone what community empowerment can look like and how it can function, and it inspired hope that the break in the community was not beyond repair.

Practicing Democratic Decision-Making

Circles can also transform our collective practices. By expanding how we understand democracy and put it into practice, Circles function as strong allies for community voices. Circles create a space in which each voice is heard with equal attention and respect. Decisions are made by consensus, which means that no interest or point of view is ignored. Decisions made in Circle are much more democratic than those made by debate-and-vote majority rule. In systems of voting, the majority can be indifferent to the needs or interests of the minority. They can get away with making no effort at all to understand or address minority concerns.

By contrast, decisions made by consensus integrate everyone's point of view. Even if only one person sees things differently, his or her view counts. It is factored into the decision-making, since consensus requires that every interest be heard and respected. This is, of course, a good and just way to be, but there are also practical reasons for working this way. Each person brings a wealth of knowledge and experiences to the process. We cannot afford to dismiss anyone's contribution. His or her perspective could hold the key to a solution no one else saw or could prevent us from overlooking something important. Obviously, dissenting views challenge us to see the whole situation differently, and this may be exactly what we need. In turn, consensus decisions must meet the needs of all participants in order to earn their support. The more a community uses consensus decision-making, the more fully democratic the community will be.

People often assume that reaching group consensus is too difficult or time consuming. And some folks have had bad experiences. Attempts to come to a consensus have, in fact, resulted in paralysis because people could not agree. Making a decision by a simple vote is faster and easier, no question. However, the outcome is not as good. Nearly half of those involved could be convinced that the choice was not the best. Will they be able to support the decision, or will they be tempted to stand on the sidelines and wait for it to fail? However the "losers" respond, majority-rule decision-making runs the risk of splitting communities. Over time, the same majority tends to win, and the same minority tends to lose.

As for the doability of the process, reaching consensus in a Circle can actually be done quite readily. It is not as difficult as many people think. For example, while Barry Stuart served as a judge in Yukon, Canada, he used Circles for hundreds of criminal cases. Some of these cases were very serious, including murder, rape, and the sexual abuse of children. Everyone who had a connection to the crime participated in these Circles: victims, offenders, their family members, community members, as well as justice officials. People had intense emotions and profound differences on all sides. Yet these Circles regularly came to a consensus about what an appropriate sentence should be.

Circles can do this because they take the time to lay the foundation before participants try to work toward a consensus. Specifically, Circles embed decisions within a shared vision based on values. They spend hours building relationships, and they commit to hearing every perspective fully. Given this strong base of community rapport, it is much less likely in Circles for opposing views to dig in and block a decision just to make a point. People understand each other

Golden Thyme Coffee is a community-based business owned by African-Americans Mychael and Stephanie Wright in Saint Paul, Minnesota. Hosting speakers and community events on a regular basis as well as providing a friendly and comfortable space for meetings and community organizing, Golden Thyme Coffee has played—and continues to play—a significant role in revitalizing the neighborhood and community. These are important considerations for planners, and Circles are an innovative way to support these dimensions of community life.

enough and care about each other enough to want to work together. Circle members feel safe and respected, which allows them to take risks in reaching out to each other. They can yield when necessary, and they can also dare to be creative.

Together, then, Circle members approach an unknown, namely, the best outcome under the circumstances. Circles do not have to force people to seek solutions that meet the interests of all the participants. The participants themselves want this because of who they have become together. In Circles, the oppositional, conflict stance morphs into a quest for mutual good. As a value, being inclusive is deeply rooted in human beings. In a well-functioning community, excluding someone or some perspective is very disturbing. It does not feel good. Once a sense of community takes hold, people want to work things out in a way that is good for everyone.

Even when a Circle simply cannot find a solution that meets all interests, it can still come to a consensus. Circles instill values that kick in when the group gets stuck. First, Circle members are committed to caring about each person's well-being. Second, Circles insist that no one be marginalized. Together, these values create a commitment to the community. In this environment, participants become more flexible and less fixed about what they must have.

As a result, Circle members will modify or even set aside their own interests when this seems necessary. If someone else's interest simply cannot be put aside without doing harm to the person, the others understand the realities involved. They see why. In yielding their own interests, they know that their views have nonetheless been heard, that others have understood their concerns, that the others care about their interests, and that the group will take every opportunity to support them as well.

In other words, Circles shift our priorities from getting what we want as separate individuals to supporting each other as a community, so that we all benefit. We may not all get everything we hoped for. However, each one can be assured that the outcome will balance everyone's interests in the best way possible according to the collective wisdom of the group.

In short, Circles make it possible for us as a society to make more decisions by consensus, particularly at the community level. Even in very complex modern communities, Circles can facilitate a more direct democracy. As planners continue to introduce Circles into the public sphere, citizens can build their skills as community members. They can then carry these skills into other areas of their lives. Through the simplicity of Circles, a much deeper democracy takes hold and spreads out. It gives us hope in change, because all our voices can play a role that matters in the process.

Cultivating Mutual Caring

Clearly, a Circle way of practicing democracy goes well beyond forming strategic political or economic alliances. It involves more than making sure that every voice is heard and represented in a decision. As we just saw in the dynamics of coming to consensus, knowing that we belong to a larger community changes how we behave. Our priorities shift from "me" to "us" and "I" to "we." We need to feel that a larger community cares about each member—that what happens to us matters to others. Circles cultivate this collective caring in many ways. Then they infuse this caring into the decision-making process.

To start, Circles invite people to show up as whole human beings. No part of us is excluded from the dialogue. We do not have to be ashamed about feeling strong emotions, for example. It is okay to cry. Nor are we discouraged from drawing on our spirituality, as long as we do not push our views on others. In Circles, we are not expected to present ourselves as "finished products." The "work in progress" approach to sharing experiences is much more effective in connecting with how others are most likely to feel.

Circles use personal storytelling to gather collective wisdom. By sharing our struggles, we create space for our best selves to emerge. In the safety of this space, people frequently drop their masks and defences and open themselves to connecting with others. Participants see themselves in one another and feel bonds of kinship. The decisions that the Circle then makes occur in an atmosphere of care and concern.

Caring and generosity are natural in human beings. A lot of caring is out there, just waiting to be expressed. Unfortunately, we have suppressed caring in communities. Whether from fear, stress, or just plain busyness, we retreat into our separate worlds. Still, the caring is there, latent in communities. Many people express a desire to help others who may be struggling, yet they say that they are often afraid to reach out. They fear that they might be overwhelmed by someone's needs or that what they have to offer might not be enough to make a difference. By addressing these inner obstacles, Circles give communities a way to access our latent powers to care for each other.

In a Circle, the responsibility for helping is shared, so that no one feels overwhelmed. The dynamics of Circles make it obvious that each contribution counts; small efforts can make a big difference. Circles provide a structure that encourages offers of help but also allows the helpers to set reasonable limits on what they do. Because Circles bring people together who have diverse skills, backgrounds, and interests, Circles integrate pieces of support from multiple sources in an organic way. The help grows naturally from the group. The result is a whole network of helping that is greater than the sum of its parts.

Members of all sorts of communities acknowledge a large reservoir of untapped goodwill and wisdom—just waiting to help those who are struggling.[2] Circles tap this potential. Helping one another is one of the best ways to build strong communities.

Sharing Responsibility

Circles build communities in other ways as well. Participants hold each other accountable for what they do—not in a harsh but in a caring way. Without accusing, shaming, or blaming anyone, Circles show members how their conduct affects both others and the group as a whole. In a Circle, the profound interconnectedness of our lives becomes visible, much more than it normally is. The values of the Circle then support people in changing their behavior, so that they no longer hurt others, especially those closest to them.

At the same time, the Circle shows how the larger community affects each individual. The values of the Circle encourage the community to take responsibility for these effects. If the impact is negative, then the community must be willing to change. Because Circles bring together such a diverse group, they offer a collective approach to making whatever changes need to occur. All the gifts and creativity of all the participants converge to craft changes and to see them through. As in a good, healthy marriage, the practice of sharing responsibilities becomes the loom on which we weave the fabric of community.

～

Democratic decision-making; mutual caring; sharing responsibility: these are core skills that people need to build communities, and Circles help us cultivate them. By using Circles, planners lay the ground for a healthy community. As Circles support a community's growth, spaces open for creativity. Ideas and solutions emerge that no one imagined before. In Circles, people express a generosity toward the community that might otherwise go unexpressed. This is because Circles create spaces for giving and receiving that simply do not exist in ordinary public processes. Because Circles are rooted in the values that define healthy relationships, they not only strengthen existing relationships but also build new ones. These relationships make the community what it is. By using Circles, planners usually discover that their work has contributed to the life of the community far beyond the goals of a specific project.

CHAPTER FOURTEEN

Renewed Liquor Licenses Violate the Sanctity of Bear Butte

BY VALERIE TALIMAN

The following story was written by an esteemed Native journalist and posted on the Web site of the Indian Law Resource Center. This case, like so many cases involving sites sacred to Native Peoples, shows how profoundly our current planning practices are not adequate to address complex issues. This dramatic conflict over land use stems from different relationships to the land, cultural and historical differences, polarized relationships, long-standing and unresolved historical grievances, and a struggle to defend basic human needs and rights. Our current practices are not working and will not work in this case, and as a result, justice is not being served.

BEAR BUTTE, South Dakota — Ignoring the cultural and spiritual rights of Native peoples, the Meade County commissioners recently approved renewed liquor licenses for four bars that have raised controversy because of their proximity to Bear Butte.

Indian nations and their supporters no doubt will continue the struggle to protect this sacred site facing off against business owners who cater to the Sturgis Motorcycle Rally, attended by more than 500,000 people last year.

But for thousands of years before Sturgis was a town, more than thirty tribes have made spiritual journeys to Bear Butte to fast, to pray, to pick medicines, and to teach their families the importance of perpetuating traditional ceremonial ways.

The Lakota, Dakota, Nakota, Northern and Southern Cheyenne, Northern and Southern Arapaho, Ponca, Osage, and Kiowa nations traditionally have ceremonies at Bear Butte in the summer months. But in recent years, these ceremonies have been disrupted by intrusions from the nearby Sturgis Motorcycle Rally and the construction of large outdoor amphitheaters that sell hard liquor and blare loud music toward the mountain where Native people are attempting to pray in solitude.

Developers promise to build "the biggest biker bar on Earth" within two miles of Bear Butte with a huge amphitheater for outdoor concerts and a campsite large enough to accommodate 30,000 bikers.

Despite continuing protests from Indian nations, churches, civil rights groups and even Sturgis residents, the Meade County Commission once again renewed liquor licenses for four controversial establishments.

Bear Butte is one example of numerous attacks across the country on Native peoples' rights to practice their spiritual beliefs in privacy and without disruption. This is not merely a cultural and spiritual concern. It is a matter of human rights, recognized in the United Nations Declaration on the Rights of Indigenous Peoples, the UN International Covenant on Civil and Political Rights, and the International Labor Organization's Indigenous and Tribal Peoples Convention (ILO Convention No. 169).

Article 7 of the UN Declaration on the Rights of Indigenous Peoples provides that "Indigenous peoples have the right ... to maintain, protect, and have access in privacy to their religious and cultural sites." In addition, Article 25 provides that "Indigenous peoples have the right to maintain and strengthen their distinctive spiritual relationship with their traditionally ... occupied and used lands ... and to uphold their responsibilities to future generations in this regard."

The UN Declaration spells out the legal and moral obligations of countries, including the United States, to respect and promote the human rights of Indigenous peoples—particularly the right to maintain, protect, and have access in privacy to their spiritual and cultural sites. This fundamental human right is at risk with the newest alcohol and concert hall developments taking place at Bear Butte. The UN Declaration recognizes these rights, and Native peoples call upon the United States to fulfill its obligation to protect Indigenous peoples' right to continue their spiritual practices at Bear Butte.

Photo by Valerie Taliman

Valerie Taliman, an enrolled citizen of the Navajo Nation, is a highly sought-after independent consultant in Native media and social justice issues. She is President of Three Sisters Media and former Communications Director for the Indian Law Resource Center. She is a former publisher, editor, and radio producer whose work has focused on environmental justice issues for nearly twenty years. She is a columnist for Indian Country Today, a foremost Native-owned newspaper. She served as co-chair of Amnesty International's Indigenous Peoples Task Force and on the organizing committee for the Native Peoples/Native Homelands Climate Change Conference and Montana's 2006 Conference on Race. She also served on the board of directors for Montana Conservation Voters and the Montana Women's Foundation. For many years, Ms. Taliman has worked with tribes in the West and Northern Plains to protect sacred sites and human rights. Contact her at valerietaliman@gmail.com

In reading this story—and there are, as we said, countless others like it—we are challenged to think of how we might be able to use the

Circle process to address such deep conflicts and come to more balanced, respectful, and just outcomes. Certainly the Circle process provides a way to take a more inclusive approach and to minimize power imbalances. Conflicts over land use are typically intense. When these conflicts are compounded by a long, unaddressed history of harms, racial animosities, and injustices, the challenge to find better ways of working through the conflicts becomes paramount. Otherwise, as in this case (to date), the existing methods perpetuate the existing patterns, which fall far short of justice.

CHAPTER FIFTEEN

Doing Justice: Planning at a Time of Planetary Transformation

Public planning is where the abstract concept of justice becomes real life. Planners make decisions every day that intimately affect people. Our planning work can have life-or-death consequences. It also affects the justice or injustice that a community experiences. Here are some of the issues that community planners routinely face:

- How do we balance private and public interests?
- If we design traffic flow this way, will people be more or less safe? Will it increase or decrease the likelihood of fatalities?
- What is the best way to get energy for our community?
- Will an industrial plant pollute, and if it will, which communities will be affected? How does the nature of these communities influence our decision about what to do?
- Do we build a coal burner to get energy, and if so, where do we build it?
- Where do we build new, mass-transit trolley lines, and where shall we locate the stops?
- Will we allow a hog farm or oil rigs—or biker bars—to be built in spite of vehement opposition from neighboring communities?
- Shall we make planning decisions that violate nation-to-nation treaties?
- Which schools and neighborhoods get cleaned up and opened first after a flood?
- Who gets forcibly removed from their homes and sent vast distances away for "the common good"?
- Into whose neighborhood shall we send our garbage?
- Where shall we build a sorting plant for our recycling?

- Where shall we put a transition house for ex-offenders?
- How can we promote local community gardens?
- What do we do when, while building a new mall, we discover that the site is an ancestral burial ground?
- Will a community decide to return land that was wrested wrongly from its Original People? If so, in what condition will the land be returned?
- When Native and First Nations purchase land to be included as part of their protected homelands, what response will the planning commissions in the area have to their land reclamation and consolidation initiatives?
- If the cheapest land is near major power-line stations or toxic waste sites, is this where we build a school, especially for children from poorer communities?
- If arsenic is discovered in the soil of an entire community, how do we plan the clean up? Whose properties do we detoxify first?
- When we discover that the groundwater has high levels of toxins that are causing birth defects across species, what do we do? Again, is our choice of action or inaction linked to which communities are most affected?
- If a development project will destroy some natural habitat, what is our response? How do we determine the importance of natural spaces and non-human species to the community?
- Who speaks for those of the natural world—the air, water, rocks, fish, birds, plants, trees, and animals? Is their well-being our collective concern? Do they have a say?
- How can we as a community reduce our footprint on the planet?
- How can we lessen our role in causing global warming and climate change?

Clearly, planning issues run the gamut—from local to global, from historical to current to future, from health to recreation, from mundane to ethical, cultural, philosophical, and spiritual. Moreover, planners often find ourselves conflicted in discussions concerning the public interest. What weight should the will of the majority carry

Where to place a power station and where to run the big transmission lines: these are the kinds of challenges and controversies that planners face and that require new thinking and new approaches. Planners are often caught in the middle. How are decisions concerning these unwanted facilities influenced by the socioeconomic composition of the community and its relative political influence?

How do we handle our waste? This is a constant challenge. This recycling plant located near a middle class neighborhood was defended in preference to a garbage burner. Whose neighborhood will now get the garbage burner?

in this situation? How about the rights of the minority? How do we make a decision about something as objectionable as a hazardous waste site? In many rural communities across North America, wind turbines are being built, often in spite of intense local opposition. Is a policy of this nature unjust, or is it simply a reflection of the broader needs of society? Such debates are complicated. Rural populations have limited political influence due to their decreasing numbers, while the larger society is predominantly urban.

There will always be debates of this nature. We as planners have a role in these debates and in choosing the best ways to resolve them. Our challenge is: How can we most effectively leverage the role we have? How can we engage our work in ways that pull with rather than against our best values and the best interests of society?

Fortunately, social policies are changing, because we are changing. Communities all over the world want a justice that has been largely missing from their lives, and we want justice to shape our relations with the natural world as well. We as planners play critical roles in the planet-wide changes that are occurring. One of our challenges is to figure out how we can be at the nexus of doing justice, both in rectifying harms of the past and in doing justice as we move into the future. How can our planning work increase the experience of justice for individuals, communities, groups and peoples, and the natural world?

Circles provide a powerful means to do this, and for all the reasons that stem from the very nature of Circles. We will name four.

Doing Justice by Agreeing on Values

Our response to planning questions depends on our values. Someone's business plans or housing project might bring us together in Circle, but we soon realize that values lie at the core of any decision we make. Do business, profits, and power make the decisions? Or do questions of justice, respect, fairness, or reverence for life have a place in the process as well?

For example, if the soil in a community is toxic from arsenic, we have to decide which areas to clean up first. One value system sets priorities around power, wealth, and political connections. The landholdings of those privileged in these ways would be cleaned up first. By contrast, another value system places priority on protecting those who are most vulnerable and who are our future: babies, children, pregnant women, mothers, and families. This value system would put a priority on cleaning up schools, day care centers, hospitals, playgrounds, and neighborhoods where the greatest numbers of children live.

The two choices send different messages about our values and priorities. So it is with every decision: we go to our values to make our choices, and whatever we decide reveals our values.

The Circle process is grounded on values, and it begins with discussing values before it tackles anything else. Without going into specifics, Circles take us straight to the heart of things—the core of what is at stake. Once we come to an understanding about our values, it is much easier to agree on a course of action. In a Circle process, the issue is no longer, for example, whether or not to do justice, especially since we may each think about justice differently. Instead, if a group agrees on including justice as a shared value, then they also come to understand what each person means by it. The question then is: How might this understanding of justice guide us in this situation? Naturally, it could guide us to resolutions in many ways, not only one.

Doing Justice by Including All Voices

According to a Circle worldview, every aspect of creation has equal value and importance. Every person has unique gifts to offer. The assumption behind Circles is that our collective wisdom is vast and that we can access it most effectively when we feel safe and respected. Each voice tells us something about the whole that we need to hear, because we all depend on the whole to survive. This is why Circles are so committed to listening to every voice until it is truly heard. For all our sakes, we cannot afford not to listen.

Yet, as we have said, being so inclusive goes against many—if not most—Euro-based institutions. So many of our habits have been shaped by exclusion, not inclusion. No wonder people often feel awkward when they first use the Circle process in contemporary society. Yet at the same time, the values of Circles run deep in us, because they are the values we need to have good relationships. Their wisdom resonates. In our experience, we find that many people intuitively use Circle values, in spite of the structures they might be working in. As a result, many people respond quickly and positively to the Circle process.

Moreover, given the state of the world, a case could be made that excluding people from decision-making has not been successful. In a narrow frame, it has given a few people wealth and power. But in a historical and global frame, it has not created peace, justice, or sustainable ways of life. It has allowed for exploitation, oppression, and many imbalances. If we factor in the costs to individuals, to entire Peoples, to other species, and to the planet, limiting decision-making to a few has been a disaster.

Climate change is a good example. The business decisions that have led to climate change over the last century were made by the top executives of corporations with the support of government leaders around the world. The global public has not been included in these decisions. Today, many of those who study climate change say that only a radical restructuring of our national and global societies can avert environmental collapse—if, indeed, it is still preventable.

Because of the scope of change we must make, some climate-change thinkers are calling for a radical democracy. In this crisis, we all need to be on board. The stakes could not be higher, and the task seems overwhelming. We need to support each other in taking steps as quickly and as effectively as we can. And we need to pool our energies, knowledge, and creativity to figure out what to do and how to do it. This is not a time to be exclusive. If we do not all change, all of our lives will be threatened. Scientists know things the public does not, but every citizen must do things differently to effect changes on a nation-wide, planet-wide scale. The challenge is to engage all our voices in the dialogue as we shift our entire way of life.

No process is more suited to meeting this challenge on a community level than Circles. We can envision a movement to hold Circles around the world to address this global crisis. From families, schools, communities, and neighborhoods to businesses, organizations, prisons, and religious groups: climate-change Circles can bring us together to mobilize our energies. And we may be in for a surprise. We may come together in Circles because we are scared for our planet and our descendants, but we may also experience a profound transformation of consciousness along the way. We might discover dimensions of who we are that have not had forums for expression, and we might find trust growing in who we can be together.

Doing Justice by Seeking Common Ground

When we come together and speak our truths, what then? Our personal experiences are vastly different, and our histories differ as well. We do not agree about many things, and we can be quite passionate about our differences. Here again, values are central to how we respond. An adversarial, win-lose response is based on the value of exclusion. The contest is about which differences to exclude.

What kind of response does the value of inclusion offer? The whole book is about this, since Circles are rooted in inclusion. What we want to discuss here is how this response does justice to all sides by first seeking common ground. An adversarial response does not do this, because it assumes common ground simply does not exist. In assuming this, though, the adversarial response comes very close to denying the other's humanity, since our humanity is something we clearly have in common.

A Circle philosophy assumes that there is always common ground to be found. Among humans, our values can help us find what we have in common based on our humanity. For example, none of us can last long by ourselves; we need others. And, no matter who we are, if we want good relationships, we need to express certain values, such as respect, mutuality, honesty, compassion, and patience. As human beings, we have these realities in common.

The more we find common ground to stand on, the more we can accept each other's differences. Finding common ground is, in fact, critical to being able to accept what is not common among us. The fear of not belonging to a group makes differences seem threatening. We are afraid that we will not belong if we deviate too much from those around us. Circles address this fear from the start by finding common ground in shared values. The more we work from what we share, the easier it is to value our differences. As the deep-seated fear of differences eases, the urge to reject those who are different to prove our allegiance to a group diminishes as well.

Reassured that we belong no matter what—no matter who we are or what we think—we feel safe enough to explore how we differ. Finding common ground is not about pretending that we have no differences, "papering over" them, or rejecting them. Quite the opposite: it is about engaging our differences to our mutual advantage. Common ground gives us ways to be together with differences— even to be stronger because of them.

Granted, differences can be hard to accept. To consider the typically difficult case, how can we embrace the perspectives of those who have perpetrated harms? Most of us would rather not see them, much less listen to them. We put perpetrators away in prisons or, in some countries, execute them. On memorials, we name individual victims but not individual perpetrators. Yet offenders have stories to tell—stories that reveal things about the society and culture we all live in. If we want to work toward justice, we need to hear all the

The natural world has paid the greatest price for human activities, which have led to deforestation, species extinction, pollution, and now climate change.

stories, so that our view of who we are together can be balanced and complete. If something is leading some of us to perpetrate harms against others, we all need to understand these dynamics, because we all are connected to the same social systems. They affect us too.

On the assumption that common ground exists, then, we can start looking for it. In and of itself, this process is good, because it is about meeting the basic needs we each have. Common ground does not mean that we all have to be the same or think the same way. Seeking common ground is about finding the ground we share that serves the collective without sacrificing any individual or group in the process. Otherwise, if some are forced to sacrifice for the benefit of others, then the collective is not served. To function well and be sustainable, the collective has to be balanced in all directions. The more it is balanced, the more those involved will experience it as just.

Unfortunately, appeals to the common good have been used to justify processes that have overrun the rights and interests not only

of individuals but also of entire groups. Sometimes this is an economic issue. Wealthier communities often have a stronger voice at
city hall. Sometimes this is a racial issue. The relationship between
white people and people of color tells this story, and the case of Bear
Butte in the previous chapter is just one example. Given the racism
that has permeated our collective histories, people of color often get
nervous when white people appeal to the common good. They know
whose good has been served and whose good has been sacrificed.

This misuse of the concept is not, though, what we advocate. Good
that comes to white people at the expense of people of color is not
common good. It is the opposite: one-sided, partial, exclusive "good."
In fact, it is not good at all but harmful. It makes society unjust, and
that is not healthy for anyone.

Clearly, adversarial processes have undermined our awareness of
common ground and common good. They have also undermined
our trust that what we have in common can help us organize our lives
in ways that benefit us all. Common good is always win-win, and yet
we often doubt that this is attainable.

These issues give us yet another view of why Circles pose such a
significant paradigm shift. Circles challenge us to rethink all these
concepts. Is there ground that we share? How can we find it? How
can we build trust in what we share when trust has been so deeply
broken? Can we draw on what we have in common to create a life
together that is truly good for all of us?

When we explore these questions in Circles, Circles help us stay
mindful of a two-way motion: how individuals and groups affect the
collective, and how the collective affects individuals and groups. The
call to be inclusive comes from the side of individuals. The call to
seek common ground comes from the collective. At the core, they
are the same. They are both about justice.

Doing Justice by Being in a Good Way
with All Our Relations

Finally, Circles are based on a belief that, at a deep heart level, every
human being wishes to be in good relationship with others. Because
of this longing, we share the core values on which good relationships

depend. We all know, for example, that respect builds relationships and disrespect hurts them. We know that a balance in giving and taking—justice—is necessary to keep relationships healthy. "No justice, no peace."

These same values apply to how we have good relationships among us as peoples and with the natural world. The entire philosophy of Circles assumes a profound interconnectedness in the universe. Again, this is a core truth among ancient and Indigenous teachings. And it is why it is not good to exclude anyone from the decision-making process or its outcome. We are all part of each other's reality. Our well-being is tied to the well-being of every other part of the universe. The more we are aware of this, the more we will strive to act in balance and harmony with others and with the natural world.

Modern science since Einstein has come to many of these same conclusions about the nature of the universe. Today, biology and physics assert that everything is interconnected. We—scientists and citizens—have learned the hard way that we cannot take things apart and work on them independently without affecting the whole. Our fates are profoundly intertwined. Just as Circles value the unique gifts that each person brings to the process, so, too, does modern biology hold that diversity is essential to the well-being of all life. Differences give us creativity and richness. They are also a source of strength and resilience. Modern knowledge meets ancient wisdom.

Most Western institutions do not operate on these assumptions, though. They simply are not up to speed with the realities of interconnectedness. They function from a European-based worldview that became outdated over a century ago. The idea of interconnectedness is one of the most ancient and universal truths that we as a species have known. Though we seem to have lost sight of it for a time, Circles can help us remember. They can help us relearn how to be in a good way with all our relations.

Focusing these ways of doing justice on planning, using Circles can build a positive awareness of relatedness in communities. Circles leave the community stronger after the planning process than it was before. Planning becomes more than simply making plans. It becomes a way for the community to come together, to listen to one

another, and to take care of each other. Planning with Circles supports a paradigm shift in communities—a deep change in how we
experience each other. Collaboration, mutual support, understanding our interdependence, and practicing our relatedness in how we
plan our lives together: these are the potentials that Circles offer.

In a time so full of fear, crises, and challenges, the way of Circles
is a way of both change and hope.

❧

Endnotes

Introduction

1. Oren Lyons, "Land of the Free, Home of the Brave," in *Indian Roots of American Democracy*, ed. José Barreiro (Ithaca, NY: Akwe:kon Press, Cornell University, 1992), 32–33. See also: Bruce E. Johansen, *Forgotten Founders: How the American Indian Helped Shape Democracy* (Harvard and Boston, MA: The Harvard Common Press, 1982) and Bruce E. Johansen, *Debating Democracy: Native American Legacy of Freedom* (Santa Fe, NM: Clear Light Publishers, 1998).

Chapter 2: Why Engage Communities?

1. Richard Neustadt and Ernest May, "Thinking in Time: The Uses of History for Decision-Makers" (New York: Free Press, 1986), 274, 106; quoted in John F. Forester, *The Deliberative Practitioner: Encouraging Participatory Planning Processes* (Cambridge, MA: MIT Press, 1999), 19.

2. Ernest J. Alexander, *Approaches to Planning: Introducing Current Planning Theories, Concepts, and Issues,* 2nd ed. (Newark, NJ: Gordon and Breach Publishers, 1992), 73.

3. Sherry R. Arnstein, "A Ladder of Citizen Participation," *Journal of the American Institute of Planners* (JAIP) 35, no. 4 (July 1969): 216.

4. See: Susan S. Fainstein and Scott Campbell, 2003; John Forester, 1989; Forester, 1999; Judith E. Innes, 1995.

5. Elster in Tewdwr-Jones & Allmendinger, 2003: 210

6. Fainstein and Campbell, 2003: 175.

Chapter 5: Different Types of Circles for Different Uses

1. John Braithwaite, "Youth Development Circles," *Oxford Review of Education* 27 (2001): 239–52.

Chapter 7: Getting Started: How to Use a Talking Circle in a Planning Process

1. This chapter is adapted from chapter 8 in Kay Pranis, *The Little Book of Circle Processes: A New/Old Approach to Peacemaking* (Intercourse, PA: Good Books, 2005).

Chapter 10: Planning the Healing Lodge

1. In Canada the term First Nations refers to the Indigenous Peoples of Canada.

2. The Canadian Association of Elizabeth Fry Societies (CAEFS) posts on

their Web site the following mission statement: "CAEFS is an association of self-governing, community-based Elizabeth Fry Societies that work with and for women and girls in the justice system, particularly those who are, or may be, criminalized. Together, Elizabeth Fry Societies develop and advocate the beliefs, principles and positions that guide CAEFS. The association exists to ensure substantive equality in the delivery and development of services and programs through public education, research, legislative and administrative reform, regionally, nationally and internationally." http://www.elizabethfry.ca/

Chapter 11: Why Circles Are Such a Good Idea: The Benefits and Potentials of Using Them in Planning

1. Juanita Brown and Sherrin Bennett, "Mindshift: Strategic Dialogue for Breakthrough Thinking," in *Learning Organizations: Developing Cultures for Tomorrow's Workplace,* ed. S. Chawla and J. Renesch (Portland, OR: Productivity Press, 1995). This article can be read in full online at the World Café Web site: http://www.theworldcafe.com/articles/Mindshift.pdf.

Chapter 12: Not All Clear Sailing: Challenges and Cautions

1. Margaret J. Wheatley, "Leadership Lessons for the Real World," *Leader to Leader Magazine,* Summer 2006. This article can be read in full online at: http://www.margaretwheatley.com/articles/leadershiplessons.html.

2. For more information about the political philosophy of Thomas Hobbes, see: Thomas Hobbes, *The Leviathan.* Oregon State University has put this classic text in political philosophy on their Web site. It can be copied and pasted at: http://oregonstate.edu/instruct/phl302/texts/hobbes/leviathan-a.html#INTRODUCTION, accessed 28 August 2009. It is also available for copy and paste at: http://www.constitution.org/th/leviatha.txt, accessed 28 August 2009.

3. For more information about the political philosophy of Han Fei Tzu, see: Burton Watson, translator, *Han Fei Tzu: Basic Writings* (New York: Columbia University Press, 1996).

4. *E: The Environmental Magazine* XX, no. 1, (January/February 2009): 23–24.

Chapter 13: Strengthening Communities: How Circles Promote Community Health

1. See: Kay Pranis, Barry Stuart, and Mark Wedge, *Peacemaking Circles: From Crime to Community* (Saint Paul, MN: Living Justice Press, 2003), 145.

2. Kay Pranis, "Building Transformative Justice on a Foundation of Democracy, Caring and Mutual Responsibility" in *Justice Reflections: Worldwide Papers Linking Christian Ideas with Matters of Justice,* Issue 11, 2006.

Circle Prep Sheet for a Talking Circle

The following summary is modified from a draft of a "Circle Keepers Manual" put out by Roca, Inc. (Chelsea, MA, 2004).

Identify

- The co-keepers
- The purpose of the Circle
- Who will be invited
- How the invitation will be extended

Plan the specifics of the Circle

The keepers put together a plan for the Circle by answering the following questions:

- What time?
- Where?
- What will we use as a talking piece?
- Will we have a centerpiece? If so, what will we put in the center?
- What will we do for opening ceremony?
- What question or process will be used to generate values and guidelines for the Circle?
- What question will be used for an introduction or check-in round?
- Is there a need for further relationship building before getting into the issues? If so, how will that be done?
- What question(s) will be used to begin the dialogue about the key topic?
- What further questions might be useful if the group is not getting deeply enough into the issues?
- What closing ceremony might be used?

Create a list of the materials and items that will be needed

This list may include, for example, items for a centerpiece, talking piece, paper plates and markers for values, and readings.

Determine how the keepers will share responsibilities

Remember that the Circle outline is a guide, not a rigid map. The process is flexible and responsive to what emerges from the group.

Identify your personal strategies for centering and focusing before the Circle begins

APPENDIX 2

Training and Further Information about Circles

Planners who would like to consider hosting a Circle training are invited to contact the authors:

Jennifer Ball: Telephone:(519) 496-8366
                      Email:jball01@hotmail.com

Wayne Caldwell: Telephone:(519) 824-4120, ext. 56420
                      Email:waynecaldwell@hurontel.on.ca

Kay Pranis: Telephone: (651) 698-9181
                      Email: kaypranis@msn.com

Additional information about Circle work can be found on the Living Justice Press Web site:

www.livingjusticepress.org

The Living Justice Press Web site includes a list of Circle keepers, trainers, community members, and professionals from any number of fields. Judges, school principals, teachers, law-enforcement, professors, parents, planners, administrators, business people, prison staff, and concerned citizens: these are some of the Circle folks listed who have experience with the Circle process and its wide range of uses. They have agreed to serve as a resource for Circle work, both for newcomers and for those who have questions or needs as they go along. Feel free to call them to talk about Circles and to discover who is conducting Circles in your area. The list is organized by state and region. On the Living Justice Press home page, click on "Who Can I Talk With About Circles?"

 APPENDIX 3

Resources: Writings and Web Sites

Writings

Alexander, Ernest J. 1992. *Approaches to Planning: Introducing Current Planning Theories, Concepts, and Issues.* 2nd ed. Newark, NJ: Gordon and Breach Publishers.

Allmendinger, P., and Mark Tewdwr-Jones, editors. 2002. *Planning Futures: New Directions for Planning Theory.* London: Routledge.

Arnstein, Sherry R. 1969. "A Ladder of Citizen Participation." *Journal of the American Institute of Planners* (JAIP), 35 (4): 216–24.

Baldwin, Christina. 1994, 1998. *Calling the Circle: The First and Future Culture.* New York: Bantam Books.

Ball, J., W. J. Caldwell, and K. Pranis. 2007. "Using Circles to Build Communication in Planning." *Plan Canada,* 47 (1): 47–49.

Boyes-Watson, Carolyn. 2008. *Peacemaking Circles and Urban Youth: Bringing Justice Home.* Saint Paul, MN: Living Justice Press.

Fainstein, Susan S. and Scott Campbell. 2003. *Readings in Planning Theory (Studies in Urban and Social Change).* 2nd ed. New York: Wiley-Blackwell.

Fisher, Roger and William Ury. 1981. *Getting to Yes: Negotiating Agreement without Giving In.* New York: Penguin.

Fitzgerald, Maureen. 2006. *Corporate Circles: Transforming Conflict and Building Trusting Teams.* Vancouver, BC: Quinn Publishing.

_____. 2006. *One Circle: Tapping the Power of Those Who Know You Best.* Vancouver, BC: Quinn Publishing.

Forester, John F. 1999. *The Deliberative Practitioner: Encouraging Participatory Planning Processes.* Cambridge, MA: MIT Press.

_____. *Planning in the Face of Power.* 1989. Berkeley: University of California Press.

Harris, Thomas A. 1969. *I'm Okay, You're Okay.* San Francisco and New York: Harper & Row.

Innes, Judith E. 1995. "Planning Theory's Emerging Paradigm: Communicative Action and Interactive Practice." *Journal of Planning Education and Research,* 14(3): 183–89.

Isaacs, William. 1999. *Dialogue and the Art of Thinking Together: A Pioneering*

Approach to Communicating in Business and in Life. New York: Doubleday Currency.

Neustadt, Richard and Ernest May. 1986. *Thinking in Time: The Uses of History for Decision-Makers.* New York: Free Press.

Pranis, Kay. 2005. *The Little Book of Circle Processes: A New/Old Approach to Peacemaking.* Intercourse, PA: Good Books.

_____. 2006. "Building Transformative Justice on a Foundation of Democracy, Caring and Mutual Responsibility" in *Justice Reflections: Worldwide Papers Linking Christian Ideas with Matters of Justice,* Issue 11.

_____. 2006. "Healing and Accountability in the Criminal Justice System: Applying Restorative Justice Processes in the Workplace." This speech given at the 2006 Symposium of the Cardozo Journal of Conflict Resolution titled: "Restorative Justice: Choosing Restoration Over Retribution." The text can be found in *Cardozo Journal of Conflict Resolution,* 8(2): 659-676 (available electronically on LexisNexis or Westlaw, url: http://www.cojcr.org/vol8no2/659-676.pdf; or in hardcopy form at your local law library.

Pranis, Kay, Barry Stuart, and Mark Wedge. 2003. *Peacemaking Circles: From Crime to Community.* Saint Paul, MN: Living Justice Press.

Rosenberg, Marshall B. 1999. *Nonviolent Communication: A Language of Compassion.* Del Mar, CA: PuddleDancer Press.

Ross, Rupert. 1996, 2006. *Returning to the Teachings: Exploring Aboriginal Justice.* Toronto: Penguin Books Canada, Reprint.

Simpson, Brenda J., & Associates. 1999. *Building Stronger Communities Learning Circle Feedback Guide.* For more information, contact Brenda Simpson & Associates, Web site: http://bsimpson.ca/, accessed 28 August 2009.

Stone, Douglas, Bruce Patton, and Sheila Heen. 1999. *Difficult Conversations: How to Discuss What Matters Most.* New York: Viking Penguin.

Thalhuber, Patricia and Susan Thompson. 2007. *Building a Home for the Heart: Using Metaphors in Value-Centered Circles.* Saint Paul, MN: Living Justice Press.

Wharf, Brian, and Brad McKenzie. 1998. *Connecting Policy to Practice in the Human Services.* Oxford and New York: Oxford University Press.

Wheatley, Margaret J. 2009. *Turning to One Another: Simple Conversations to Restore Hope to the Future.* 2nd ed. San Francisco: Berrett-Koehler Publishers.

Zehr, Howard. 1990, 1995. *Changing Lenses: A New Focus for Crime and Justice.* Scottdale, PA: Herald Press.

_____. 2002. *The Little Book of Restorative Justice.* Intercourse, PA: Good Books.

Web Sites of Interest

We chose the following Web sites because they offer interesting information about various types and uses of the Circle process.

Boys to Men Circle at St. Louis Park Public School, St. Louis Park, Minnesota

http://www.slpschools.org/afam.html The Boys to Men Circle is a group for African American boys in grades 9–12 at St. Louis Park Senior High. It is a weekly support and advocacy group where the students meet to talk about school successes, barriers, needs, etc. It is run in a restorative justice circle practice that teaches respectful communication and active listening. The goals of the group are to increase academic performance and social skills and to support students with personal issues.

Circle Dialogue Process Training, Delaware County, Pennsylvania

http://www.circledialogue.com/ Restorative Justice Community Circles offers Circle trainings as well as various programs and applications of Circles in the Philadelphia and Delaware County area. The site includes explanations and experiences of Circles as well as links.

The International Association of Public Participation (IAP2)

www.iap2.org/ IAP2 is a global membership association seeking to promote and improve the practice of public participation in relation to individuals, communities, governments, corporations, and institutions.

Living Justice Press, Saint Paul, Minnesota

www.livingjusticepress.org/ Living Justice Press maintains an informational Web site about the Circle process. LJP's site includes a regional list of people who have experience with Circles and are available as a resource (click on "Who Can I Talk With About Circles?"). These "Circle people" can assist in different capacities, from advice to facilitation ("keeping") to providing training in Circles.

Circles of Peace, Nogales, Arizona

www.circlesofpeace.us Circles of Peace is a domestic violence treatment and prevention program that uses a restorative justice Circle approach to reduce violent behavior in families.

Partners in Restorative Initiatives, Rochester, New York

www.pirirochester.org Partners in Restorative Initiatives, located in western New York, works with schools, courts and communities to instill restorative practices through education, advocacy, training and facilitation. Much of their restorative work is conducted in Circles, and they offer trainings in Circles as well.

PeerSpirit Inc., Langley, Washington

http://www.peerspirit.com/circle-training.html This is the site of Christina Baldwin, who has been advocating the use of Circles for many years.

Restorative Justice and Circles, Blog by Kris Miner

http://circlespace.wordpress.com/ This blog by Kris Miner, executive director of the Saint Croix Valley Restorative Justice Program, includes nearly fifty articles about restorative justice and the use of Circles. The site is updated regularly, as Kris Miner shares stories from her diverse experiences with using Circles.

The Restorative Way, Minneapolis, Minnesota

http://www.therestorativeway.org/ This Web site, created by the late Chuck Robertson and maintained by Oscar Reed and Jamie Williams, provides in-depth information about the Circle process and the meaning of the circle from an Indigenous perspective. It also includes information about the use of Circles in schools.

Rudi Askim Writing

http://www.magma.ca/~raksim/learning_circle.htm As the URL indicates, this work focuses on learning Circles, less on the Circle process itself and more on how learning Circles can be integrated with a larger planning program.

Saint Croix Valley Restorative Justice Program, River Falls, Wisconsin

http://www.scvrjp.org This restorative justice program offers Circle trainings and focuses particularly on using Circles in schools and with teens, especially to promote safe teen driving.

Index

A

accountability: shared in Circles, 10, 43, 100–101, 119, 127, 154

adversarial processes, 99, 119, 136, 144, 165–66, 168; and win-lose, 94, 99, 165; vs. win-win, 94, 168

African Americans, 6, 140–41, 151

Arnstein, Sherry, 26, 95, 146

arrow metaphor, 145

B

balance: in Circle process, 42–43; and consensus, 40–41; in decision-making, 33, 40–41, 98, 133, 145; of diverse views, 8, 19, 135; and equality, 35–36; individual and collective, 117, 148, 152; inner and outer, 36; and justice, 167, 169; and Medicine Wheel, 42–43; as a principle, 34–35; and "third parties," 149

Barter, Dominic, 115

Bear Butte, 155–57, 168

"being in Circle," 33: as a mindset, 104–105

Bell, Wilma, 141

Bennett, Sherrin, 119

"best selves," 33–34, 36, 121, 153

Bluewater case, 48, 82–87, 149

Braithwaite, John, 59

Brown, Juanita, 119

Bullard, Robert, 140–41

C

Caldwell, Wayne, 31, 175

Campbell, Scott, 26

caring: keeper's role of, 40, 133; mutual, 152–54

centerpiece, 75

ceremonies (opening and closing), 37–38, 47, 74–75, 80, 101, 110, 113

chaos and order, 124–25

challenges to Circle-use, 123–46: documentation, 134–35; lack of experience, 129–31; false hopes, 135–36; fear of the unexpected, 129–31; a new process and unfamiliar roles, 13–14, 43, 123–33, 137, 149; number of participants, 135; as risky, 82, 128–29, 131, 136; terminology, 126–27; time constraints, 133–34

Chandler-Rhivers, Gwen, 6–7, 10, 17

change, 124: and Circles, 60, 116, 120, 122, 127, 129, 154, 170; and hope in, 152; and planning as managing, 15, 21, 136; and power to, 136, 142

Circles, 14, 27, 48, 176: and acknowledging emotions, 24; balance among parts of, 42–43; as balancing individual and collective, 117; benefits of, for planning, 33, 115–22; and "best selves," 121; and cautions about, for planners, 12, 123–42; for celebration, 58, 90–91; characteristics of, 41–44, 48; and citizen participation, 14, 96, 98–99; for community building, 3, 60–61, 93, 147–54; and community members, 83, 87, 149–52; compared with conventional processes, 13–14, 19–20; for conflict resolution, 12, 48, 58, 94–95, 116–17; and consensus, 115–16, 149–52; convening, 46–47; as creating

145–46; in planning processes, 5,
19, 26, 108; as solution to "mob
rule," 8; within a group, 84

E

effectiveness: criteria for, 128
Einstein, Albert, 169
emotions: as expressing values, 21,
26; around planning processes,
19, 21–26; and stories, 26, 30
environmental justice, 140, 157
equality, 5, 9–11: and balance, 35; in
Circles, 35, 37, 40, 99, 107, 129;
and talking piece, 99
Euro-dominant thinking, 8–9, 169:
and democracy, 7–9, 11, 137, 139,
164
exclusion: vs. Circle's inclusion,
115, 164–65; consequences
of, 138–41, 144, 164–65; from
decision-making, 138–42, 144,
151, 164–65, 169; and democracy,
6–7, 10; habits of, 164; of have-
nots, 26; of minorities, 6

F

Fainstein, Susan, 27
feedback: in Circles, 81, 106–107; in
planning, 141–42
First Nations, 8–9, 16, 96, 109–113,
139, 160, 171
following up after a Circle (stage
4), 47–48, 81
food: use of, in building relationships, 46, 75–76, 106–107
Forester, John, xi–xii, 27
Franklin, Benjamin, 137
freedom, 5, 9
French, Randy, 16, 92, 105, 131, 133

G

Gardner, John W., 146
Goffman, Ethan, 140

government: models of, 4–5; philosophy of, 4
guidelines, 30–31, 38, 40–41, 44, 46,
76–79, 84–85, 145: in planning
contexts, 98–103
grassroots processes, 17, 25, 144

H

Han Fei Tzu, 138, 145
Haudenosaunee Confederacy: and
practice of democracy, 9, 137
Healing Lodge, 109–115
Hobbes, Thomas, 138, 145
holistic view: as Circle's approach,
48, 119–20; of conflicts, 144–45;
vs. hierarchical control, 123, 125
human nature, 138, 142–46. *See also*
"best selves."

I

ideals: vs. practices, 5–11
inclusivity, 119, 139, 151: and Circles,
30, 33, 72, 99, 106, 115, 151, 158;
and consensus, 40–41, 151; creates a better process, 17, 27, 111;
and doing justice, 146, 164–65;
as ideal of democracies, 5; leads
to better decisions, 95–96, 111,
146; paradigm shift to, 142–43;
in public planning, 26, 142–43;
and redistribution of power, 26;
as a value, 151. *See also* decision-
making, democracy
Indigenous Peoples and cultures:
and Circles, 14, 32–36, 40, 54, 63,
70; and injustices to, 64, 139–41;
and land struggles of, 139–41,
155–58; and Medicine Wheel,
43; and sharing food, 46; and
teachings of, 34–36, 40, 43, 145,
169; and UN Declaration on the
Rights of Indigenous Peoples,
156; and values, 169

bottom up, 116; for social justice, 121–22

P

paradigm shift, 13, 125: Circles as introducing, 123, 126–27, 137; to inclusion, 142–43, 168, 170

Peacemaker of the Haudenosaunee Confederacy, 9

peacemaking Circles, 13, 33, 38–39: philosophy of, 99; values of, 58. *See also* Circles

philosophy: about conflicts, 143; affects decision-making, 4; affects planning processes, 4; of Circles, 16, 33, 61, 72, 94, 99, 123, 131, 136–37, 166; Circles promote shift in, 15, 31, 88; political, 138–39, 145

planners: and applying elements of Circles, 98–108; basic job of, 20–21, 27–28; as Circle participants, 131–33; Circles promote philosophical shift for, 15, 31, 88, 104; and codes of democratic ethics, 28; and control of planning outcomes, 8; and concerns about Circle use, 123–46; and Euro-based solutions, 8; and fear of public involvement, 8; and frustration with conventional public processes, 24; how Circles can help, 29–31, 88–108; and including all voices, 19, 26–27, 29, 107, 146; and increasing justice, 162–63; and issues of who to include, 142; limited power of, 28, 136; and listening to stories, 27–28, 105–106; as managing change, 21; and parameters of role, 141–42; pressures on, 19; and promoting diversity, 19; and relation with

communities, 28–29, 83, 98–99; and role of, in debates, 159–63; and use of less intense or complex Circles, 89–94

planning: collaborative, 26–27; defined, 20–21; with democratic values, 26–27; and injustices, 139–41; and issues of, 159–63; leadership in, 27; potentials for using Circles in, 88–108; reasons to use Circles in, 29–31. *See also* change, Circles, decision-making, planning processes

planning processes: affected by philosophy of government, 4; aim to be inclusive, 26, 146; challenges facing, 19; and Circles, 3–4, 14–17, 27, 29–31, 61–62, 70–81, 88–108, 123–37; community involvement in, 28–29, 83, 91–92, 96, 148–49; and diversity, 19; emotions surrounding, 19, 21–26; goal of, 4; including those most affected by, 139–41; and need for more inclusive, 26, 142–43, 146; for public good, 21; and public participation in, 29–31; and relationship building in, 105, 107–108; and role of stories in, 105–106; and talking Circles, 70–81; types of Circles useful in, 61–62; and values, 16–17, 100. *See also* Circles, citizen participation, decision-making, planners, planning

Pranis, Kay, 83, 87

preparing for a Circle (stage 2), 45–46, 48, 58, 73–76

privilege, 6, 8, 17, 138–39, 142–43, 163

problem-solving: and Circles, 3, 48, 118–19; and hearing the story, 19, 28

Author Information

Jennifer Ball, Ph.D., RPP, MCIP

Jennifer Ball holds a Ph.D. in Rural Studies, with a focus on Sustainable Rural Communities, from the University of Guelph in Ontario, Canada. She has conducted research on issues of intercultural communication in professional planning, conflict management, storytelling, and rural land use planning. Her current research relates to women and peacebuilding, with a focus on Uganda, East Africa. She also specializes in narrative research methodologies.

Jennifer has taught courses in International Development at Conrad Grebel University College, University of Waterloo, Ontario, Canada. She has also conducted workshops on peacebuilding in Kenya, East Africa. Jennifer is an accredited land use and community development planner and worked for several years as a rural planner in Ontario, Canada. She currently consults with a number of research projects at the University of Guelph.

Jennifer was born in Zambia and has spent over thirteen years living and working in East and Southern Africa (Zambia, Botswana, Kenya, Uganda, Tanzania)—with Indigenous and Aboriginal communities (the Basarwa)—in community development, microenterprise development, market research, and peacebuilding.

Telephone: (519) 496-8366
Email: jball01@hotmail.com

Wayne J. Caldwell, Ph.D., RPP, MCIP

Wayne Caldwell is a Professor in Rural Planning at the University of Guelph in Ontario, Canada. He also has a career-long affiliation with the County of Huron Department of Planning and Development.

Wayne has lectured across North America on the future of rural communities. His primary focus has been on planning and change in rural and agricultural communities. He is an active researcher and practitioner in the area of farmland preservation, rural conflict resolution, public participation and facilitation, governance of nutrient management, and community-based approaches to economic and environmental issues. He has published four books including *Farmland Preservation: Land for Future Generations.*

Wayne is a founding member and past Chair of the Ontario Rural Council. He is also a founding member of the Huron Stewardship Council, and the Lake Huron Centre for Coastal Conservation. He was appointed by the Ontario Government to Chair the Provinces Nutrient Management Advisory Committee, and he is President of the Ontario Professional Planners Institute.

Telephone:(519) 824-4120, ext. 56420
Email:waynecaldwell@hurontel.on.ca

Kay Pranis

Kay Pranis is a national leader in restorative justice, specializing in peacemaking Circles. She served as the Restorative Justice Planner for the Minnesota Department of Corrections from 1994 to 2003. Before that, she worked six years as the director of research services at the Citizen's Council on Crime and Justice. Since 1998, Kay has conducted Circle trainings in a diverse range of communities—from schools to prisons to workplaces to churches, from rural farm towns in Minnesota to Chicago's South Side.

Kay has written extensively on restorative justice and the peacemaking Circle process. With Barry Stuart and Mark Wedge, she wrote the foundational book on Circles: *Peacemaking Circles: From Crime to Community*, which is soon to be in its fourth printing. This book has been published in Ukrainian and will soon be out in Russian as well. She also wrote *The Little Book of Circle Processes: A New/Old Approach to Peacemaking* (Intercourse, PA: Good Books, 2005). This book is also used extensively in Circle trainings.

Kay has presented many papers on peacemaking Circles and restorative justice in the United States, Canada, Australia, and Japan. Over forty of her articles on restorative justice and Circles have been published in newsletters, magazines, and professional journals around the world.

Telephone: (651) 698-9181
Email: kaypranis@msn.com

About Living Justice Press

A 501(c)(3) tax-exempt, nonprofit publisher on restorative justice

Living Justice Press (LJP) publishes books about social justice and community healing. We focus specifically on restorative justice and peacemaking, and within this field, we concentrate our work in three areas.

First, we publish books that deepen the understanding and use of peacemaking Circles. Circles help people deal with conflicts and harms in ways that promote justice and "being in a good way" as a way of life.

Second, because restorative justice draws directly from Indigenous philosophies and practices, we publish on Indigenous ways of understanding justice. These ways have to do with learning "how to be good relatives"—not only with each other but also with the peoples of the natural world.

Third, we publish the voices of those "in struggle" for justice. Our books seek to apply what we have learned about healing harms between people to the larger and more systemic challenges of addressing harms between peoples. Through our publishing, we join in working toward justice between peoples through paths of education, exploring how to rectify harms, and transforming our ways of being together. According to restorative justice, this journey begins with hearing the stories—especially from those whose voices have not been heard—and finding out from those who suffered what it would take to "put things right."

We want to thank all those who support Living Justice Press by buying our books, using them for classes, making financial donations, as well as donating time through volunteer work. We want to express our special thanks to Cathy Broberg, Dave Spohn, and Wendy Holdman for their most skilled and generous work on our behalf, enabling us to produce books of such consistently high quality inside and out. We are also grateful to the staff of Sheridan Books, Ann Arbor, Michigan, for their high standards in service and printing. We continue to exist through the support of everyone in the Living Justice Press community. We are deeply grateful. Thank you!

Books from Living Justice Press

On the Circle Process and Its Uses

Peacemaking Circles: From Crime to Community by Kay Pranis, Barry Stuart, and Mark Wedge, ISBN 0-9721886-0-6, paperback, 271 pages, index.

Building a Home for the Heart: Using Metaphors in Value-Centered Circles by Pat Thalhuber, B.V.M., and Susan Thompson, foreword by Kay Pranis, illustrated by Loretta Draths, ISBN 978-0-9721886-3-0, paperback, 224 pages, index.

Peacemaking Circles and Urban Youth: Bringing Justice Home by Carolyn Boyes-Watson, ISBN 978-0-9721886-4-7, paperback, 296 pages, index.

Doing Democracy with Circles: Engaging Communities in Public Planning by Jennifer Ball, Wayne Caldwell, and Kay Pranis, ISBN 978-0-9721886-6-1, paperback, 200 pages, index.

On Indigenous Justice

Justice As Healing: Indigenous Ways, edited by Wanda D. McCaslin, ISBN 0-9721886-1-4, paperback, 459 pages, index.

On Addressing Harms between Peoples

In the Footsteps of Our Ancestors: The Dakota Commemorative Marches of the 21st Century, edited by Waziyatawin Angela Wilson, ISBN 0-9721886-2-2, oversize paperback, 316 pages, over 100 photographs, color photo insert, index.

What Does Justice Look Like? The Struggle for Liberation in Dakota Homeland by Waziyatawin, ISBN 0-9721886-5-7, paperback, 150 pages (approx.), index.

We offer a 20% discount on orders of 10 books or more. We are delighted to receive orders that come directly to us or through our Web site. Our books are also available through amazon.com, and they can be special ordered from most bookstores. Please check our Web site for announcements of new LJP books.

We are expanding to carry some titles from other publishers as well. We selected these books because they have played a significant role in our journeys in restorative justice. Either they are not well known or they may be hard to find. So we invite you to check them out on our Web site.

Order by phone, fax, mail, or online at:

2093 Juliet Avenue, St. Paul, MN 55105
Tel. (651) 695-1008 • Fax. (651) 695-8564
E-mail: ljpress@aol.com
Web site: www.livingjusticepress.org

Acclaim for Doing Democracy with Circles
continued from page ii

"This book has value for citizen involvement in planning as well as conflict resolution and negotiation. The wide range of applications is impressive."

—Thomas Daniels, Professor in the Department of City and Regional Planning at the University of Pennsylvania

"This text is a wonderful introduction to circles for planners. The stories provide very helpful examples. They are inspiring and help show various directions for possible applications. The text provides a thorough treatment and covers every major area that needs to be addressed. It is very readable and tremendously inspiring. It is a much-needed text.

"I'm just coming from the Metropolis conference in Halifax— Metropolis is a research and community network that addresses issues related to immigration. This is a huge field in which circles have enormous potential to contribute.

"I really enjoyed this . . . and am excited to get training and start working more in this area."

—Heidi Hoernig, Assistant Director, Office of Research Opportunities, McGill University